Committee of the Regions thesis competition

1996-2003

CoR Studies I-2/2004

Brussels, September 2004

This study has been elaborated by the Unit for Policy Analysis, Studies & Inter-institutional Legislative Planning of the Committee of the Regions.

A great deal of additional information on the European Union is available on the Internet. It can be accessed through the Europa server (http://europa.eu.int).

Cataloguing data can be found at the end of this publication.

Luxembourg: Office for Official Publications of the European Communities, 2004

ISBN 92-895-0338-6

Foreword

Every year since 1996, the Committee of the Regions has organised a thesis competition, open to young doctors of law, economics, and political and social sciences. Its aim is to strengthen dialogue with the European academic world and to raise the profile of the Committee of the Regions among a wide academic audience.

A topic for research is set each year according to the political priorities of the Committee of the Regions and the European Commission. The winning theses aim to help deepen the academic discussion on the fundamental issues for local and regional authorities, such as devolution, European governance, trans-European cooperation, enlargement, etc.

In recent years, the political and institutional situation has provided particularly fertile ground. We have seen the enlargement of the European Union to ten new Member States and the drafting of a Treaty establishing a Constitution for Europe. These matters have been the subject of major research projects and of numerous academic comments and publications in European universities. They have given rise to new developments, which are at the heart of the concerns of local and regional authorities and therefore of considerable interest to the Committee of the Regions.

The provision in the draft Constitutional Treaty for the local and regional dimension to be taken into account in the future institutional architecture implies new responsibilities for the Committee of the Regions. By supporting academic research by awarding prizes to the best young European researchers in its various areas of activity, the Committee hopes to enhance its increased role in the implementation of the principles of subsidiarity and proportionality in the drafting of Community policies.

Since the thesis competition was established, the Committee of the Regions has already awarded prizes to 18 young researchers, the authors of outstanding doctoral theses on the role of regions and cities in Europe. The purpose of this publication is to present the prize-winners' research. I hope that it will lead to the prize-winning theses of the CoR's annual competition reaching a wider audience.

Peter Straub
President
of the
Committee of the Regions

Table of contents

1996/1997

THE EUROPEAN UNION: HOW SHOULD LOCAL AND REGIONAL AUTHORITIES PARTICIPATE IN THE INTEGRATION PROCESS?

Chairman of the jury

Ms Claude du Granrut (FR), Member of the Regional Council of Picardy, Deputy Mayor of Senlis

Theses submitted

NUMBER OF ENTRANTS	LANGUAGES		COUNTRY
30	7	German English Finnish French Italian Portuguese Swedish	9	Germany Austria Belgium Finland France Italy Portugal Sweden United Kingdom

Winners

First prize:

Dr Anders Östhol (SV), *Political integration and cross-border region-building in Europe*, Department of Political Science, Umeå University

Second prize:

Dr Robert Pochmarski (AT), *Implementation problems of European Community law in the federal state*, Institute of Public Law, Political Science and Administration, Karl-Franzens University, Graz

Special mention:

Dr Kai Hasselbach (DE), The *Committee of the Regions in the European Union*, Faculty of German and European civil and business law, Friedrich-Schiller University, Jena

*

*   *

Anders Östhol, Umeå Universitet

Political integration and cross-border regional cooperation in Europe

My prize-winning 1996 thesis concerned the influence of political integration in Europe in fostering conditions for transnational, cross-border cooperation. New regions are in practice formed when cross-border cooperation is developed furthest. The most important conclusion was that the ongoing political integration is of great importance in providing scope for local and regional cooperation. There is a connection between EU membership and the rise of cooperation between municipalities and regions. Regions are formed when local and/or regional bodies network in innovative ways in large cross-border areas.

However, for cooperation to make an impact, it is necessary for the regions on either side of a border to have similar powers. In other words, formation of a region presupposes a certain measure of autonomy. The conditions for different types of cross-border activity are shaped by the institutional factors promoting integration and the degree of operational integration. Cross-border regions acquire greater freedom of action through the creation of new regions, the allocation of greater financial resources at regional level, an expanded area of responsibility or better formal safeguards for autonomy. However, these conditions are also influenced by the intensity of operational exchanges across the border. For instance, if many commuters cross a national frontier to and from their work, a demand will arise for better cross-border administration with the capacity to solve problems that arise.

Analysis shows that there has been a steady rise in the number of cross-border partnerships ever since the Second World War, from 1947 onwards. One major cause is that the climate for region creation has become much better. This is borne out by the fact that cooperation between local and regional authorities is more frequent and far more advanced within the EU compared with non-member countries. Joint projects are more frequent in EU Member States, with the exception of the cooperation that has developed within the framework of the Nordic Council and on the borders of Switzerland which in most cases did not originate in EU initiatives. The countries where cooperation was most prevalent all belonged to the heart of Europe. German regions were by far the greatest participants in joint projects, followed by the French, Italian, Austrian and Swiss regions.

The pace has been particularly fast in connection with the deepening and widening of European cooperation, e.g. through the 1987 Single Act and in connection with earlier enlargements. For instance, cross-border cooperation was rare in Greece, Portugal and Spain before they became members of the EU. There was a dramatic increase in this development in eastern Europe after 1989-90, only a short time after the fall of the communist governments there. Both Tacis and PHARE are examples of programmes whose structure has been inspired by many features of Interreg and which are intended to pave the way for new members of the EU.

Forms of cross-border cooperation

Different types of arrangement lay the foundations for cooperation at sub-state level. It is impossible to frame common rules at supranational level, since that would be like creating new supranational bodies. A number of other methods have instead developed along voluntary lines.

The paradox is that it is primarily national governments which negotiate agreements at international level - not regions or the EU Commission. Consequently the scope for intra-state negotiations with border regions eager to cooperate with their foreign counterparts is a decisive factor. Formally regions cannot do more than their responsibilities allow. At the same time it is clear that they can do more than their official remit provides for in, for instance, bargaining and encouraging on their own initiative various interested local and regional players to share the costs of transregional cooperation. There are also a number of other informal channels for boosting opportunities for independent regional initiatives. Inter-regional organisations such as AEBR (Association of European Border Regions) and AER (Assembly of European Regions) have been successful in highlighting the importance of cooperation across national frontiers as a way of developing regions and in stressing that the potential impact is closely connected with greater regional autonomy.

Clearly regions wishing to cooperate across national frontiers cannot rely entirely on national governments as regards involvement in cross-border matters. Nonetheless central governments play a key role in fostering a favourable climate for cooperation through bilateral and multilateral agreements and cross-border national committees.

We know from experience that cross-border cooperation often starts with an inter-state committee set up to solve cross-border problems, e.g. the opening up of new communication routes. Major infrastructure projects create excellent opportunities for operational cooperation since they break down natural frontiers and thereby make it easier to cross mountains, seas, rivers and valleys which previously kept populations apart. It is also essential for spatial planning to be better coordinated.

To make a real impact, it is necessary for several tiers of authority to cooperate. Local and regional schemes alone cannot deal with all the obstacles to free movement across frontiers. Tax, employment, social insurance and housing are issues that can only be tackled effectively if more than one decision-making level is involved. These matters normally do not even come within the remits of local and regional authorities. It is therefore necessary to involve several players. Here the EU Commission plays a key role in placing pressure on national governments, securing funding and actively encouraging local and regional initiatives.

It has been found that national governments have no objections to the EU shouldering responsibility for some at least of regional concerns. Individual countries do not have the same ambition as in the past to pursue an independent regional policy. Given that interdependency between several tiers of authority has been properly developed, there are no major reasons for national governments to try to obstruct the growth of cooperation arrangements at levels below the supranational and international. Indeed there are sound grounds for internal problems to be dealt with at other levels than the often overburdened central government.

The following forms of broader institutional framework are conducive to promoting cross-border cooperation:

- *Committees.* These inter-state bodies lay the foundations for cross-border cooperation by making it possible to coordinate policy more effectively in a number of sectors which otherwise impede cooperation. Often working groups are set up in specific spheres: environment, transport and infrastructure, social affairs and research and development. This is tantamount to recognition on the part of central government that barriers must be dismantled to step up cross-border exchanges.

Local and regional authorities are involved through their membership of special committees. The problem of these committees is that they are not so effective in creating the right dynamic interaction between different levels, which requires relatively few resources but has proved to have a major impact on readiness to cooperate.

- *Regionalisation*. The degree of regional autonomy is more or less clearly defined in constitutions. Federal constitutions go furthest in this matter. Federations provide formal guarantees for territorial division of powers between two formally equal units: over and above the central government, the regions or federal states. In recent years a number of pragmatic and targeted reforms have paved the way for regionalisation in several European countries without any constitutional changes taking place. Financial resources and tax revenue alone will, however, not suffice in order to achieve lasting changes. Resources and legal and political powers must be transferred to the regions if we are to be able to talk about cross-border regionalisation. One example is the setting up of democratically-elected assemblies which either represent both sides directly or, which is usually the case, indirectly represent local authorities which choose to cooperate within the framework of a union of local authorities.

In my thesis I have chosen to distinguish between unitary states and federations. Federation is still an alien concept for most countries which do not already have some federal elements. Experience shows that formal division of powers only comes about in extraordinary circumstances when a state's entire existence is threatened by war or in connection with voluntary or imposed peace agreements. In typical unitary states, such as the United Kingdom, Netherlands and Sweden, the local authority level is still far more important than the regions. One major difference is that the local authority level in these countries presents no challenge to the central government whereas federal states in federations such as Germany and Switzerland lay claim to equality in domestic policy matters and thus also make greater claims to autonomy in external relations.

The paradox is that greater powers in the areas on which regionalisation normally focuses - education, infrastructure, spatial planning and structural policy - require large-scale resources. Regions are seldom prepared to shoulder these costs themselves. Unless regions are allocated a combination of legal, political and financial powers, regionalisation will remain just a pipe dream. In other words it is probable that further steps towards regionalisation are to some extent linked with existing measures to improve conditions for pursuing cross-border cooperation. Purely national forms of regionalisation are not enough to get rid of the negative barrier effects created by national frontiers. Some form of cross-border regionalisation is necessary, i.e. in practice the same powers in external relations or at any rate the authority to conclude agreements in the spheres of internal affairs for which local authorities are responsible.

- *Supranational programmes*. During the current period the most important cross-border programme, Interreg, has a budget of around ECU 4,000 million. A number of programmes within the EU have successfully promoted cross-border cooperation. Besides Interreg, Tacis and PHARE are the programmes which focus most on cooperation. Influenced in particular by Article 10 and Interreg, cooperation has grown rapidly since the early 1990s. This increase is most apparent in the border areas between Spain and Portugal, and between France and Spain, and most recently along the border between Germany and Poland. One common factor is that these regions have started from a very low starting point. This is regarded as a good way of preparing for EU enlargement.

Gradually *policy networks* have been developed in connection with programme implementation and to some extent also in connection with the framing of policy. Projects are a natural means of generating new ideas on the right instruments for their implementation. It can therefore be hard to distinguish between lobbying and practical implementation of policy. The Interreg programme has proved uncontroversial, mainly because it is transnational and not redistributory. Programmes focus directly on cross-border situations and not on reapportioning funds from one area to another. There has therefore been no opposition on the part of governments. On the contrary, the Interreg programme has managed to combine local, regional and national resources in an innovatory form.

In the most successful cases, all decision-making levels have realised that they have shared interests. Overall it would seem that cooperation has benefited greatly from EU assistance in large areas of Europe. This drive gathered momentum only after the reform of the Structural Funds in 1988, when the budget was doubled and partnerships were introduced as a method of working with EU programmes.

Content and nature of cooperation

To date experience has shown that public authorities are the main protagonists in cooperation schemes. In the great majority of cases, organisation takes private law forms. At local and regional level, private law forms of association are roughly three times more common than public law forms. In my recent research into regional partnerships in Sweden I have found that some new players, e.g. universities, have started to play a greater role in regional cooperation and development schemes. Partnership has been far less successful in respect of involving private business. That does not seem to be the case in cross-border cooperation because of the major role played by chambers of commerce in regional cooperation, especially in Germany, France, Austria and Switzerland.

Chambers of commerce are only surpassed by local and regional authorities when it comes to cross-border contacts. Private companies played a surprisingly important role, followed by universities and colleges, and various forms of foundations. Contacts with central government authorities came far down the scale. The various types of voluntary organisations are an under-represented category. Trade unions, political parties and other political movements take a low profile.

One major experience has been that cross-border cooperation necessitates some form of interaction between different tiers. The EU has been particularly effective in creating this type of interaction and common understanding among players through acting as a third party, largely untouched by the frequent struggles between regions and central government keen on defending their own areas of authority. Without the EU's infusion of vital resources, there is good reason to believe that this positive impact would not have been forthcoming.

The most important spin-off effect so far has been that cross-border cooperation has assumed more solid forms. It has moved on from informal discussions and personal relations to more decision-making bodies. The remaining constraint is that such cross-border bodies cannot be legally based in more than one country. There is no scope for going further. Nonetheless the vision of Europe has made great progress. It is now acknowledged that cross-border cooperation at local level is important. The EU has shown that increased transfrontier exchanges at local level and on a European scale complement each other. After examining cross-border cooperation at local and regional level it is clear that such cooperation is most prevalent in the following spheres:

1) Infrastructure
2) Environmental protection
3) Cultural exchanges
4) Administrative cooperation
5) Research and development.

These areas seem particularly suited to cross-border cooperation. However, closer scrutiny of the types of activity concerned argues for caution when it comes to drawing conclusions. Joint projects cannot be expected to involve regulatory, standard-setting or monitoring activities. The types of activities to be observed show that the emphasis is largely on development and does not comprise any exercise of authority. Exchanges of information were the most common activity, followed by planning. More general activities such as network creation are, like the cross-border studies carried out, an important component in forging cooperation in the start-up phase. Across the board it is not clear at what point authority can be exercised in the networks which are set up.

Operational integration

The regularity of interaction is the most important indicator when seeking to create an operational region spanning national frontiers. Commuting to and from work is a common yardstick for operational integration. Transfrontier exchanges can be expected to have considerable influence on the identity of the population in the long term and to create demand for institutional solutions in a number of matters (employment, social insurance, taxation, etc.). Cross-border commuting is most common in the areas concentrated in the Rhine valley, for many centuries a communication link near areas constantly rent by strife along the Swiss, French, German, Belgian, Luxembourg and Dutch borders. In practice, the area connects up border regions and cities stretching from the Alps to Rotterdam and encourages a very large number of the most developed cross-border initiatives (Euregio, Regio Basiliensis, Maas-Rhein, Rhein Waal, etc.).

Switzerland had a total of 155,000 commuters (*Grenzgänger*) at the start of the 1990s. Paradoxically this country, which is not an EU member, is the commuter capital of

Europe. One decisive factor has been its demand for labour. In the space of 20 years commuting has increased by no less than 121%. A sharp increase in the number of commuters can also be observed in the EU. Between 1970 and 1990 the increase in cross-border commuting was 74% (excluding Switzerland). In the EU too labour market requirements have been reflected in the rise in commuting. Experience shows that trained workers who already have a job, as opposed to the unemployed, account for this increased mobility. To some extent, price differentials also explain cross-border mobility in that it can be profitable to buy a house and live on the other side of a border. The stretches of border with the largest number of commuters are: Lombardia-Ticino (Italy-Switzerland), Genève/Ain Haute-Savoie (Switzerland-France), Saar-Luxembourg-Moselle (Germany-Luxembourg-France), and Basle-Südbaden-Haut Rhine (Switzerland-Germany-France).

In the last few years, at any rate, the increase in commuting has been outstripped by the setting-up of new organisations for cross-border cooperation. We can conclude that operational integration is progressing more slowly than institutional integration. The reason why the border regions are at the forefront of European integration is largely the catalyst role now played by the EU. The case of Switzerland shows that transfrontier institutional integration at municipal and regional level in no way coincides with those areas where operational integration is greatest. In the slightly longer term the organisation of cross-border cooperation can reasonably be expected to stimulate greater mobility. This is one of the major challenges the future presents for the EU, along with further enlargement of its membership.

Robert Pochmarski, Karl-Franzens-Universität, Graz [1]

Implementation problems of European Community law in the federal state

1.   Introduction

As the European level has become more visible outside the academic and administrative elites, the question of the legitimacy of the European integration process has become increasingly acute. In the public debate the question of legitimacy is usually taken together with the European Union's democratic deficit[2]. The focus is on the decision-making process. In the academic debate on European integration too, legitimacy is linked primarily, indeed almost exclusively, with democracy[3]. Germany's Federal Constitutional Court is no exception; in its judgment on Maastricht it equates legitimacy exclusively with (parliamentary[4]) democracy - as mediated by the population of the state[5]. The example of Weimar shows that democracy does not by itself necessarily give rise to legitimacy. Max Weber[6] pointed out the many facets of the concept of legitimacy.

---

[1]   The author is an administrator at the European Commission's single market DG. The article is an expression of his personal opinion and is not the official view of the Commission.

[2]   See, for example, the critical discussion on the subject in Kreher/Weber-Panariello, Gedanken zum Demokratiedefizit der Europäischen Union, Traverse 1994/3, 64-88. They argue that, as a new form of political control, the EU needs democratic legitimacy on the model of the nation state.

[3]   See the special edition *National Parliaments and the European Union*, The Journal of Legislative Studies 1995/3; Classen, Europäische Integration und demokratische Legitimation, AöR 119 (1994), 238; a criticism of the fixation of the legitimacy debate on parliamentary democracy can be found in : Christiansen, Gemeinsinn und Demokratiedefizit, Strategien zur Optimierung von Demokratie- und Integrationsziel, in: Steffani/Thaysen (Pub.), Demokratie in Europa: Zur Rolle der Parlamente (1995), 50 et seq.

[4]   Max Weber showed that democracy and parliamentarism are not identical and that parliamentary structures do not on their own guarantee democratic substance - Weber, Parlamentarisierung und Demokratisierung, in: Kluxen (Pub.), Parlamentarismus, 27, (1969).

[5]   BVerfGE 89, 155 [156] Maastricht.

[6]   Weber, Wirtschaft und Gesellschaft, chapter III, 5th edition, (1988).

Luhman linked legitimacy with a sociological theory of procedure[7]. The concept of legitimacy itself may be open to criticism, as it is difficult to measure[8].

The legitimacy and public acceptance of European integration are determined by a variety of factors. In the process of European integration both the decision-making phase and the implementation phase have an impact on the legitimacy of the project. In oversimplified terms, it may be assumed that legitimacy and public acceptance are decisively influenced by participation, transparency and efficiency. All three factors concern the development phase of Community law; only the latter two concern the implementation phase. These three factors also have the advantage that, on the one hand, they are considered to exhibit deficits and, on the other hand, that they are measurable. These factors do not necessarily go hand in hand[9].

This dissertation concentrates on the implementation process; within the trio of legitimacy factors referred to above it concentrates on efficiency in relation to the implementation phase. The weighting of legitimacy factors in the framework of the complex system of the European Union is necessarily different from that in the Member States; there would moreover be no point in using an (ideal) state model as a basis and point of comparison. The weighting of the legitimacy factors can be undertaken in accordance with a mobile system[10]. In such a system a minus rating for one factor must be balanced by a plus in another area. The last two intergovernmental conferences (Amsterdam and Nice) have highlighted the limits to improvement in the fields of participation and transparency. Expectations of an operational single market are high and will rise still further with the introduction of the euro. At the current stage of integration

---

[7]   "A political system can […] ensure that its decisions are always taken as binding; […] This by no means requires universal consensus, or total standardisation or politicisation of society. […] Such a system has a good chance, as it exploits its own-decision-making opportunities, to change public expectations. If it succeeds in this, it legitimises itself through procedures." - Luhmann, Legitimation durch Verfahren, 252f, (3rd edition, (1978)).

[8]   "The concept of legitimation, in short, has no clear operational meaning, nor agreed upon empirical referent. It is difficult to disentangle operationally from other motives for obedience. (...) It leads research away form substantive legal doctrine and towards unlikely hypotheses of attitudinal and behavioral change merely because something is law. Nor does it capture social facts not equally capturable by theories of compliance premised on rationality" - in *Hyde*, Legitimacy in the Sociology of Law, Wisconsin Law Review, 1983, p. 426.

[9]   The trade-off between efficiency and democratisation can be taken as read. See, for example, Mantl, Repräsentation und Identität, 320 et seq., (1975); Steffani, Zur Problematik von Effizienz, Transparenz und Participation, in: Steffani (Pub.), Parlamentarismus ohne Transparenz, 17 et seq. (1973).

[10]   Wilburg, Entwicklung eines beweglichen Systems im bürgerlichen Recht, (1950).

efficiency therefore (still) seems to be the decisive factor in determining the legitimacy of European integration.

Whilst in Germany there is a long tradition of debate on the issue of the federal state and integration (a classic expression of this is Ipsen's concept of the Community's "country-blindness"[11]) the focus of attention has been mainly on structures for participation and influence or on reform of the federal state[12]. There does however seem to be a degree of "blindness" with regard to the implementation of Community law in federal states. In federal systems the federal "länder" regions are closely involved in implementation. This increases the likelihood of unequal implementation. Federal systems of government therefore constitute a challenge for European integration, even in the implementation phase. This paper highlights the connection between participation in the decision-making phase of European legislation and subsequent implementation. The dividing line between the two phases proves to be a narrow one. This hypothesis is developed and illustrated in the light of the conflict over the television without frontiers directive. Community and national instruments are analysed in terms of implementation deficits. The structural boundaries of national instruments are highlighted. From this it follows that greater account has to be taken of Community instruments. A further possible development of the law would be to balance the proposed right of the regions to bring an action before the Court in the event of a breach of the Treaty with the right to bring an action against the regions themselves on the same grounds.

Only if a balance is struck between rights and obligations will the desired objective be achieved: a result which preserves autonomy and is compatible with the Treaty, whilst strengthening the legitimacy which European integration needs.

2. Basic considerations concerning the implementation of Community law in the federal state

This chapter sets out the basic considerations concerning - the mainly national - implementation of Community law. The ECJ has ruled that every Member State is entitled to allocate powers in whatever way its deems fit and to implement a directive by

---

[11] Ipsen, Als Bundesstaat in der Gemeinschaft, in: Caemmerer/Schlochauer/Steindorf, FS Hallstein, 248, (1966).

[12] See: Hilf/Stein/Schweitzer/Schindler, Europäische Union: Gefahr oder Chance für den Föderalismus in Deutschland, Österreich und der Schweiz?, VVDStRL 53 (1994); Epiney, Gemeinschaftsrecht und Föderalismus: "Landes-Blindheit" und die Pflicht zur Berücksichtigung innerstaatlicher Verfassungsstrukturen, EuR 1994, 301 mwN.

means of measures adopted by regions or local authorities; this devolution of powers does not however absolve the Member State of its responsibility for ensuring that the provisions of directives are implemented accurately and without restriction in national law[13].

The EU's implementation standards are illustrated by the judgment of the Irish Supreme Court in the Meager case[14]. In Ireland implementation takes place mainly in the form of legislation amending the law with only "negative parliamentary supervision" and the possibility of *ex nunc* abrogation. The virtual exclusion of national parliaments from the development phase of Community law and the implementation of directives by means of executive legislation are relevant to the questions of the legitimacy and public acceptance of Community law. The quasi-administrative role[15] of national and regional parliaments is relevant both to the fundamental question of the separation of powers and to the relationship between Community and Member State. It would of course be wide of the mark to apply ideal concepts such as the separation of powers[16], which even at national level are not fully realisable[17], to the Community. On the other hand, a comparison should be drawn between the quasi-administrative role of parliaments in the downstream phase of the legislative process with their participation in the upstream process. The Meager case shows that, regardless of all the efficiency arguments, leaving implementation effectively to the executive and allowing the elected parliament only a

---

[13] ECJ C-227-230/85.

[14] Supreme Court (Ireland) Case 127/1993 *John Meager ./. Minister for Agriculture and Food, Ireland and the Attorney General,* [1994] ILRM, 1-28; Analysis: Travers, The implementation of directives into Irish law, ELR 1995, 103-110; Hogan, The Meager Case and the Executive Implementation of European Directives in Ireland, MJ 1995, 174-186; *Carney, Meager v Minister for Agriculture:* An Opportunity to Angel Dust Article 29.4.5.o; ILT 1995, 187-192.

[15] In Federal Trade Commission v Rubercoid Co., 343 US 470, 487/488 (1952) Justice Jackson concluded that "[…] *quasi* is a smooth cover which we draw over our confusion as we might use a counterpane to conceal a disordered bed."

[16] "In every government there are three sorts of power: the legislative; the executive in respect to things dependent on the law of the nations; and the executive in regard to matters that depend on the civil law." - Montesquieu, The Spirit of Laws, Book XI, Chapter 6.

[17] Kreher/Weber-Panariello, Gedanken zum Demokratiedefizit der Europäischen Union, traverse 1994/3, 64-92; "The Community does not admit […] the *principle of the separation of powers* in its traditional form". *GRABITZ/Nettesheim, Art 4 Rdnr 1.;* Against analogical thinking on national constitutional law matters: Ipsen, Europäisches Gemeinschaftsrecht, 318, (1972); The impact of the Community model of organisation and powers on the Member States is difficult to assess in detail, particularly as the Member States themselves do not represent an ideal model of the separation of powers. Bernd-Christian Funk's statement that "in the long term the logical outcome of the current trend would be the end of the constitutional state" can, from, from this point of view, be fully supported. See Funk, Die Entwicklung des Verfassungsrechts, in: Mantl, *Politik in Österreich,* 706, (1992).

negative supervisory powers is highly problematic. Delegated legislation is necessary only within very narrow boundaries - e.g. as a result of European integration. Ultimately, the administrative role of national parliaments in implementation would appear acceptable only if they had a meaningful share in the development of Community law. To set against the example of Ireland, with its practically non-existent parliamentary participation and mainly administrative implementation, is that of Member States with strong parliamentary participation and limited delegated legislation - such as the Federal Republic of Germany and Austria. There are constitutional and legal arguments against a system which, as in Ireland, leaves *integration law* and thus also *integration policy* to the executive.

The paper goes on to list the Community's minimum implementation standards: requirement for precision, legal clarity, publicity and legal protection, as well as the parallelism of the implementing act, all of which are developed on the basis of the ECJ's case law. On this basis it is possible to assess individual cases to establish whether implementation by national bodies - and thus also by "länder" or regions - has been satisfactory or not.

3.   Implementation shortcomings - a constitutional problem

In order to realise a constitution - and in this sense the Community Treaties are a constitution - "standards must", as Konrad Hesse put it, "apply not only hypothetically but also in reality"[18]. In relation to the effective realisation of the single market, 1 January 1993 was merely the beginning of the process - all the more so in the light of each subsequent enlargement. The option of selective implementation therefore becomes a real challenge for integration.

This should on the one hand be distinguished from protective clauses: the *protective clauses* introduced by the Single European Act as compensation for the extension of majority voting in the Council are quite different in character from *selective implementation*. The *derogations for economies with a low level of development* contained in Article 15 of the EC Treaty and the *integrated protective clause* provided in Article 95(5) of the EC Treaty which is open to all Member States are a component of the Community legal act itself. They, like the *individual protective clause* laid down in Article 95(4) of the EC Treaty are part of the process of the development of law itself. Thus problems are highlighted during the development phase of the Community legal act.

The measures adopted in application of the integrated protection clause of Article 95 (5) of the EC Treaty are thus subject to a *Community scrutiny procedure* designed to prevent abuse. The national provisions applied in application of Article 95 (4) of the EC Treaty are subject to a *Community approval procedure*. In both cases involvement of the European Court of Justice is possible.

The three provisions referred to above are all cases of the application of the concept of *phased integration*[19]. Whilst as a pragmatic approach *phased integration* pursues the objective of progress on integration, *phased implementation* results however in disintegration. *Phased integration* may be the second best solution, but from a Community point of view, *phased implementation* is not acceptable.

A clear distinction must also be drawn between selective implementation and *ultra vires* acts and their consequences. In its *Maastricht judgment* the Federal Constitutional Court described the situation with regard to ultra vires acts by Community institutions as follows: if European bodies or institutions were to implement or develop the Union Treaty in a way which was incompatible with the Treaty as implemented in German law, the resulting legal acts would not be binding in Germany. The German state bodies would, for constitutional reasons, be prevented from enforcing those legal acts in Germany[20]. The Federal Constitutional Court ruled that the decision as to whether *ultra vires* acts have been carried out lay within its exclusive jurisdiction. Whilst in the case of suspected *ultra vires* acts there may be dispute as to whether only the European Court of Justice is empowered to declare the action null and void in the context of an action under Article 230 of the EC Treaty, or whether national constitutional courts[21] or even other national bodies are entitled not to apply the legal act, this question does not arise in the case of *selective implementation*.

---

[18]   Hesse, *Grundzüge des Verfassungsrechts der Bundesrepublik Deutschland*, Rdnr 42, 16th edition, (1992).

[19]   For this concept see Scharrer, *Abgestufte Integration - Eine Einführung*, in: Grabitz, *Abgestufte Integration - Eine Alternative zum herkömmlichen Integrationskonzept*, 1-30, (1984); Langheine, *Rechtliche und institutionelle Probleme einer abgestuften Integration in der Europäischen Gemeinschaft*, in: Grabitz, *Abgestufte Integration - Eine Alternative zum herkömmlichen Integrationskonzept*, 47-124, (1984).

[20]   BVerfGE 89, 188 Maastricht.

[21]   Thus, in connection with the dispute between the German federal government and the "Länder" on the *television without frontiers* directive, the State of Bavaria applied to the German Federal Constitutional Court for exemption from the requirement to implement the directive. This was found to be inadmissible by the court (see also footnote 25).

Selective implementation is the "new challenge of compliance"[22] or "safety net" by which the negotiating phase is extended. Extending this period for as long as possible can consequently be interpreted as maximising the benefit. The new challenge of selective implementation gives rise to sanctions, Community standards (the financial sanctions of Article 228 ECT; Francovich judgement; sanctions under Article 280 ECT) and participation in decision making by the Member States and regions. It may be concluded that participation in policy-making - regardless of the extent to which the outcome is influenced - excludes the possibility of invoking technical difficulties (in the broader sense). If there are political or (real) technical difficulties, these have to be highlighted during the policy-making phase. Moreover, they must be contained in the Community legal act itself or in a national standard confirmed by the Commission. They are to be allocated to the *legislative phase* and not the *implementation phase*. The paper analyses the extent to which vital interests and fundamental constitutional principles must be taken into account during the process of drawing up Community law. If Community legislation fails to take account of the *core area of a national constitutional principle*, the same applies in relation to the consequences as in the case of *ultra vires* acts; such acts must, however, be complied with by state bodies until their inapplicability or nullity have been established in legal proceedings. The only point at issue between constitutional and European lawyers is whether the proceedings should take place before the national or European constitutional court. In principle it may be assumed, however, that the European Court of Justice has exclusive competence. Scrutiny by a national constitutional court seems only a theoretical possibility[23], given the low probability of blatantly ultra vires acts by Community bodies. It is clear that, even if it is suspected that the integration barriers set by national constitutional principles have been overstepped[24], the national body responsible for implementation is not entitled to oppose integration on its own initiative. Only when the existence of an ultra vires act by the Community bodies has been established by the constitutional court is non-application or non-implementation

---

[22]   Weiler, *The Transformation of Europe*, Yale Law Journal 1991, 2463 et seq.; Weiler, *The White Paper and the Application of Community Law*, in: Bieber/Dehousse/Pinder/Weiler (eds.), *One European Market?* A Critical Analysis of the Commission's Internal Market Strategy, 337, (1988).

[23]   Griller confirmed the principle of supervision by Austrian bodies in such blatant cases. This can only mean the constitutional court - Griller, Verfassungsfragen der österreichischen EU-Mitgliedschaft, ZfRV 1995, 100.

[24]   The question of where to draw the integration boundaries of fundamental national constitutional principles is discussed in connection with the legal dispute over the television without frontiers directive in front of the Federal Constitutional Court (BverfG judgment of 22.3.1995 - 2BvG1/89).

legally justified[25]. The implementation phase is not the right time to raise competence-related or constitutional objections to standards established by Community law.

4. Instruments to tackle implementation deficits

This section of the paper distinguishes between Community instruments (actions brought in connection with breaches of the Treaty, proceedings for a preliminary ruling) and national instruments (substitutive execution[26]). An analysis of the relevant demarcation lines is followed by an assessment, drawing on legal and policy-making considerations, of opportunities for development. Although Article 228 of the Maastricht Treaty provides sanctions applicable in relation to proceedings in connection with a breach of the Treaty, the conclusion in the Ehlermann case, that the limits of proceedings in connection with a breach of the Treaty may be narrower than lawyers might like, still applies.[27]. However, the Commission has in some cases incorporated application of flat-rate penalties into an action brought before the ECJ, and judgments have been given imposing financial sanctions of this kind. It should, however, not be forgotten that neither the lump sum nor the penalty payment can be applied against Member States under Article 228(2). Whilst non-payment is highly unlikely, the retention of Article 192 ECT, which excludes enforcement against the Member States, is counter-productive from the point of view of effective sanctions. To set against the legal and political limits of the procedure under the EC and Euratom Treaties, there is Article 88 of the ECSC Treaty, which provides that if the state has not fulfilled its obligation by the time limit set by the Commission, or if it brings an action which is dismissed, the Commission may, with the assent of the Council acting by a two-thirds' majority, suspend the payment of any sums which it may be liable to pay to the state in question under the Treaty. No decision of this kind has ever been taken, however, which illustrates the political limitations of this procedure.

The inherent limits of the preliminary ruling procedure are determined to a great extent by the readiness of the (highest-level) national courts to make referrals. It should also be pointed out that proceedings alleging a breach of the Treaty on grounds of non-compliance[28] with the referral requirement[29] are in effect ruled out. There is also the

---

[25]   See above for the question of whether, in addition to the ECJ, national constitutional courts are also required to decide such questions.

[26]   See Pochmarski, Substitutive Powers vis-à-vis Regions. A Means to Improve Compliance with European Law? The Cases of Germany, Italy and Austria., LL.M. Thesis EUI Florence (1995).

[27]   Ehlermann, *Die Verfolgung von Vertragsverletzungen der Mitgliedstaaten durch die Kommission*, in: Grewe/Rupp/Schneider (pub.), Festschrift Kutscher, 152, (1981).

[28]   For the submission requirement see ECJ C-283/81

question of the admissibility of legal remedies against Court preliminary rulings[30]. In legal terms legal remedies against referral decisions should be inadmissible in European law[31]. Legal remedies *against the refusal to refer* should on the other hand always be admissible in order to give the European Court of Justice the greatest possible opportunity for preliminary rulings. It should be up to be ECJ to reject referrals as inadmissible *a limine* or to ensure a manageable workload by altering its procedural rules[32].

Domestic instruments for ensuring implementation of Community law are based on the classic concept of state responsibilities under international law. But, on the one hand, the integration process itself has moved far away from its point of origin and, on the other hand, the role of federalism in the Member States with regard to "external policy"[33] has been considerably strengthened[34]. Clearly instruments of this kind - for example central government supervision, federal government compulsion in Germany and substitute competence in Austria - are anachronisms, and their practical irrelevance is analysed in detail. In particular, instruments of this kind are in practice impossible to apply as a result of political inter-relationships in federal states.

---

[29] If the European Court of Justice were to find against a Member States as a result of a breach of the Treaty by one of its courts, the problem would arise as to how the judgment was to be applied. Interference by the executive of the Member State in the prerogatives of the judiciary would seem to be ruled out by the principle of separation of powers.

[30] In the de Geus v. Bosch case the ECJ ruled that Article 234 ECT is not an obstacle (ECJ C-13/61); the Supreme Court of Ireland, on the other hand, ruled in the Campus Oil case that legal recourse against referral decisions by national courts were inadmissible (CMLRev 1984, 741 with comments by Murphy).

[31] O'Keefe described the admission of legal recourse against referral decisions by the European Court of Justice as a "fundamental error", see: O'Keefe, *Appeals against an Order to Refer under Article 177 of the EEC Treaty*, ELR 1984, 104.

[32] For the question of certiorari, see Rasmussen *Issues of Admissibility and Justiciability in EC Judicial Adjudication of Federalism Disputes under Article 177 EEC*, in: Schermers et al (pub.), *Article 177 EEC: Experiences and Problems*, 379 et seq., (1987).

[33] "Writers, politicians and the course of international affairs remind us constantly that politics everywhere is connected with politics everywhere else. Through a variety of processes and channels, power is now exercised at a global level in a variety of spheres and with a bewildering variety of political effects. [...] This process of extension has had its effect not only on the empirical reality of world politics but also on the way analysts and practitioners conceive of the global arena." - Smith, *Modernization, Globalization and the Nation-State*, in: McGrew/Lewis (Ed.), *Global Politics - Globalisation and the Nation State*, 253, (1992).

[34] See the comprehensive study by Renaud Dehousse, *Fédéralisme et relations internationales*, (1991). The possibility of sub-national units being involved in the conclusion of international treaties should be considered: Austria: Article 16 Constitution; FRG: Article 32(3) Constitution; Belgium: Article 68(1) First Federal Constitution of 5 May 1993.

5. Conclusions and prospects

Given that domestic instruments are in effect insignificant, at least as regards the general run of implementation deficits, a number of proposals are called for to improve Community instruments. One possible way of making proceedings relating to a breach of the Treaty more effective - apart from allocation of resources[35] - would be to make it possible to enforce judgments of the ECJ stipulating a lump sum or penalty payment against Member States. This would however not be easy, as this could be seen as a first step away from a supranational towards a federal legal order. It would be simpler to give regions with legislative powers a privileged position with regard to the right to bring actions under Article 230 of the EC Treaty, whilst also making it possible for actions to be brought against them in the framework of Article 226. Moreover, in areas in which a representative of the federal länder has participated in decision-making in the Council under Article 203 of the EC Treaty and where the main legislative and/or administrative onus of implementation falls on a federal land, it is difficult to see why it should not be possible to bring an action for breach of the Treaty directly against the same federal land. A substantial weakness of the preliminary ruling procedure is the differing degree to which national courts are prone to make referrals. For this reason, restriction to final-instance courts should be decisively rejected. Furthermore, it should be the ECJ itself which decides on the admissibility of a decision to refer. Legal remedies against submission decisions should be inadmissible. The operation of the ECJ could be maintained by a change to the procedural rules.

---

[35] Commission Communication on the balance between the staffing and tasks of the Commission (2000).

1997/1998

REGION AND CITY: RIVALS OR PARTNERS IN A DECENTRALISED EUROPE?

Chairman of the jury

Dr Franz Schausberger (AT), university lecturer, Governor of Salzburg

Theses submitted

NUMBER OF ENTRANTS	LANGUAGES		COUNTRY	
13	6	German English Spanish French Italian Portuguese	8	Germany Austria Spain France Greece Ireland Italy Portugal

Winners

First prize:

Dr Harald Gohm (AT), *Decentralised self-organised regional development as the example of an initiative for an adjusted regional development (MIAR) in the district of Landeck*, Law Faculty, Karl-Franzens University, Innsbruck

Second prize:

Dr Anne Poussard (FR), *The Atlantic Arc - A Chronicle of Interregional cooperation*, Centre for Research on the spatial and social dimension, University of Caen

Harald Gohm, Karl-Franzens-Universität Innsbruck

Decentrally self-organised regional development, as in the example of the association "Indirect initiative for an adapted regional development in the district of Landeck" (MIAR)

Introduction

At the beginning of the 1990s, there appeared in the district of Landeck, situated in the Austrian province of Tyrol in the triangle between Italy, Switzerland and Austria, a completely new development in the field of regional development for Tyrol.

At the initiative of some committed individuals, an association was created in accordance with the "bottom-up principle" to deal with regional planning and development policy issues in the district: the association "indirect initiative for an adapted regional development", or MIAR for short. The members of the association were dissatisfied with the development concepts laid down from on high, which only rarely came to fruition, and decided to draw up targeted projects that had been developed and put into effect by specialists. Also, "thinking in a semi-circle" was discontinued. The daring step was taken to cross over the national frontier to the neighbouring regions of Engadin/Val Müstair (CH) and Vintschgau (I).

This regional initiative also aroused the interest of the Tyrolean provincial government, which tried to transfer the idea and structure of MIAR to other parts of the province; in this way regional development associations were set up in other districts. The development of the MIAR association was also observed with interest by the Austrian spatial planning conference OEROK, and this "model for decentrally self-organised regional development" was transferred to other Austrian regions.

The present dissertation examines the various legal questions and problems connected with the municipal, district and even cross-border activities of the association.

Since the regions of Austria and/or Europe are constantly gaining in importance as more and more of the powers of the nation-state are transferred upstream to Europe on the one hand and, on the other, downstream to the provinces, districts and municipalities in accordance with the subsidiarity principle, the first part of the dissertation initially examines the concept of the region from the historical, sociological and legal point of view. In particular, the connection between regionalism and federalism is discussed, as is the concept of self-organisation. Attention is also drawn to various European initiatives concerning regionalism, and the possibilities for financing regional development associations are examined. The structure of cross-border co-operation in Europe is illustrated by the ARGE ALP, the Tyrol Europaregion and the Regio Basilensis before the second part of the dissertation discusses the emergence of the MIAR association, its structure and its projects.

A lot of space is devoted to this area because of the co-ordination tasks of the MIAR association within the framework of the EU regional promotion programmes.

The greatest difficulty in drawing up the dissertation lay in the time-consuming research work, which was largely based on personal conversations with association members, regional managers, officials and politicians.

Region

A regional self-awareness is becoming apparent everywhere in Europe. It expresses itself in the most diverse forms: Starting with the cultivation of local dialect in poems, songs and plays; a greater interest in local and regional history; emphasis on regional peculiarities and interests in politics, moving on to a strong resistance against the centre and to efforts at separatism. In the dissertation, however, it has to be pointed out that views differ greatly on what makes an area a region, and that the scientific and general terminology used in connection with the concept of the region is most contradictory. This is due to the fact that regions are, on the one hand, forms of order under different designations and, on the other, are theoretical constructions. So, many authors, who may not be averse to adding their own ideological sauce to the stew, have highly divergent views on how to define the term "region".

Decentralisation by self-organisation

The age of the industrialised civilisation is marked by a powerful process of centralisation and uniformity, both in state and in economic matters. The expansion of the public sector has clearly reached its limit. This limit is, of course, firstly one of funding, but it is also one of how much things can be organised in their present form.

A number of central supply and planning systems are in crisis and public confidence in this method of overcoming social and human problems has evaporated. In the "tertiary sector" in particular, there is the problem of above-average increases in the cost of services (e.g. care for the sick and the aged, as well as for education). If these price increases are not accepted, there is a risk of deterioration in the quality and the quantity of services, and even of their disappearance from the market and/or state. However, despite this the state extends its spheres of influence apparently non-stop by constant expanding its planning and supply systems. Because of this the dependence of the individual on bureaucracies and economic conditions has already reached such a critical mass that this expansion cannot be increased further without a change of system. Since some establishments are linked both horizontally and vertically with the policy, new co-ordination problems have arisen. Without achieving their particular goals, administration - together with politics - are being cut off from the outside world. In this way the very reason for centralisation (quicker and more targeted management of social problems) has largely disappeared. The costs and the staff of this system remain, since they must be maintained.

This dissertation shows that this problem can be tackled by decentralisation. The traditional form of decentralisation is that type of organisation known as "self-government". This is all about organisational units under public law becoming institutionally independent of a direct state authority system and being given sole responsibility for running certain public affairs by the persons particularly concerned (i.e. at the most under state supervision).

The second type of "self-organisation", which is investigated in greater detail in the dissertation, represents a further form of decentralisation. It is about the voluntary coming together of citizens to provide "functional public services" such as crop tending, welfare, social assistance, preventive health care, counselling, life support, disaster relief, rescue services, national defence, civil protection and many more. "Self-organisation" differs from "self-government" firstly in its legal form (mostly civil law bodies) and secondly by having a certain spontaneity, which shows itself at least at the beginning of the development. "Self-organisation" is always a reaction to a problem. Individuals band together in "self-organisations" because they expect thereby to satisfy special needs which are denied them by other economic subjects (in particular the state). The importance and efficiency of self-organisation has long been misjudged - particularly in state-dominated systems - ("association dairy"). It was thought that the state bureaucracy alone could carry out these minor democratic tasks more rationally and efficiently. Only the Anglo-Saxon world never followed this line. Law and order was never understood there as purely a state matter. Since "self-organisation" is characterised by freedom of contract and private autonomy, one finds there a multicoloured palette of legal and organisational forms.

Financing

"Self-organisations" raise the funds necessary for their work from the most diverse sources. Funding problems have become much more acute in recent years. Members of self-organisation units often identify themselves so much with their project that they are prepared to give not only their time but also to make financial sacrifices (in the hope of being reimbursed later and in the belief that only a minimum amount is involved anyway) in order to provide public goods from which non-members quite obviously also benefit. The dissertation also mentions the problem of "free riders". These leave it up to the members to finance the collective goods from which they, though non-members, also benefit.

As regards the funding of "self-organised" regional development units, it was noted that disregarding the regions as a quasi-important administrative unit always leads to problems, since work on projects which cross municipal boundaries is always dependent on the goodwill of municipal leaders.

The MIAR association

Origin of the association

At the beginning of the 1990s, a thought process began in the Landeck district. It was recognised that there was no discussion forum for projects that crossed municipal boundaries and/or were run by several municipal authorities. There were interest groups, but solutions to problems in the regions could only come from the top down, i.e. from central and provincial authorities. A body which pointed out problems at regional level and discussed them upstream did not exist at that time. As part of the preparation of a district development programme a loosely-knit discussion group was formed, known as "ARGE area planning". This group, which consisted of representatives of Landeck employer, worker and agricultural organisations, the employment office and area planning experts, decided right from the start that their goals would be achieved not by drawing up position papers and development programmes but by identifying weaknesses and putting together priority action programmes to deal with them. The group wanted to tackle problems which were not dealt with or considered by the municipal authorities because they crossed municipal boundaries. It was recognised that further experts were necessary and it was decided to set up a council consisting of politically independent experts to discuss problems in the region and come up with a solution to them.

During an initial brainstorming session the most diverse fields of action from the areas of economic development, tourism, energy, waste disposal etc. were discussed. Special attention was paid to the future of old people in the district and it was decided to prepare a policy paper on care for the elderly. The costs for this concept came to around ATS 1 million. With the proviso that the project would always be co-funded out of the own resources of the respective beneficiary, since otherwise the project would lack relevance and focus, the municipalities of the district were brought into the process of preparing the position paper. These were surprisingly positive about providing care for the elderly. The question soon arose of how implementation of the scheme could be co-ordinated and which body should be responsible. It was therefore decided to set up a regional development association based on the structure of the original ARGE.

The dissertation notes that thanks to the particular relevance of a topic like care for the elderly, 26 municipalities, four tourist associations, all the chambers of the district, banks and also many private individuals became members of the association from the outset and the association could already boast 50 members at its foundation.

Objective

The goal of MIAR is: "to initiate appropriate regional development and adapt it to the needs of the Landeck district". This goal has been achieved above all through increased networking and/or harmonisation of the most diverse regional policy opinion and decision makers at district, provincial, and national level. MIAR's task at district level is to take over functions which are not properly performed by central bodies, existing institutions, establishments or interest groups or by the municipalities.

The MIAR association's work is very well known in the district of Landeck and has achieved a high level of acceptance by both the general public and by political decision-makers. This is due in particular to the fact that:

27

- A topic was taken up, particularly a starting project like "care for the elderly", which was of interest to all municipalities;

- The association is represented to the outside world by people who are committed, competent and known in the district;

- The association enjoys the full support of the responsible district and provincial authorities as well as the local media.

The dissertation points out that this acceptance is not by any means a foregone conclusion for a regional development association. Partner associations in the neighbouring districts of Imst and Reutte have suffered since their foundation from the problem of not being accepted by politicians or the public.

The municipalities and the regional development association

The municipalities play an essential role in self-organised regional development, since in most cases they are also directly involved in the implementation of projects. The active and supportive co-operation of the regional development association is therefore absolutely essential to the success of independent development in the region and to the achievement of development targets. But the role of the regional development association is still not recognised by some municipal leaders. This in turn has negative consequence particularly for the funding of the association, although most of the funds for the association's current work still come from the municipalities.

The association's project work

The association's project work falls into two categories:

In the case of project administration all the organisational aspects are handled by the association. The association initiates the project, selects the necessary experts and arranges funding.

In the case of project co-ordination the association steers projects which it does not actually administer itself, by using its know-how and its contacts with public bodies, for instance.

Current projects

At present the MIAR association handles the administration of over ten projects and the co-ordination of a further eight. The volume of investment mobilised by these projects is approximately ATS 27 million. The MIAR association also works in a supporting role on 32 projects. To handle this abundance of tasks, a further four female workers have been hired over the years alongside a regional manager installed since July 1995.

As regards content, projects are concerned with the fields of location marketing, local supply, technological infrastructure and the setting-up of interprovincial co-operation between the districts of Landeck (AT), Vintschgau (IT) and Unterengadin/Val Muestair (CH).

In recent years external activities have been particularly stepped up. This has involved publicising the contents of the association's work and co-operating with partner associations in Tyrol and/or across the border with regions in South Tyrol and Switzerland. As well as beefing up content information in the traditional print media, there has also been a constantly updated Internet presentation in co-operation with partner associations in the districts of Reutte and Imst.

Probably the association's biggest success in cross-border co-operation with the neighbouring regions of Engadin/Val Muestair and Vintschgau was the joint organisation of a "Three Provinces Fair". This "Three Provinces Business Fair" saw 300 exhibitors showing their products and services to over 50,000 visitors from the border regions. This was the high point of preparatory work lasting over five years which succeeded in bringing together the population through the exchange and presentation of regional products and services. Prejudices were broken down, new relationships were cemented. The fair was largely funded through the EU's INTERREG project.

One of the most recent large-scale projects was the creation of a location marketing catalogue for the promotion of a concept business park. By publishing and describing relevant location data (business areas, infrastructure, manpower supply) and tying-in and presenting successful guidance operations in an image brochure, the regions of

Tyroler Oberland[1] and Ausserfern[2] were actively marketed as an attractive business location.

In the "Via Claudia Augusta" project an old Roman road has been actively upgraded as a historical special feature and as a common denominator of the bordering regions in the fields of culture, tourism and handicrafts. Project priorities are, on the one hand, archaeological surveys and, on the other, the marketing of the Roman road as a tourist attraction. Thus, cycle tracks and footpaths are signposted all along the Roman road leading from Italy through Tyrol to Bavaria.

All regional projects receive significant funding from European incentive funds and from the provinces.

It has to be noted that in the years since the dissertation was completed, the association's project work has greatly increased in scope. This particularly applies to cross-border co-operation under the INTERREG programmes. The association could particularly enhance its acceptance by the public with such cross-border activities. Its only problem continues to be fund-raising.

---

[1]   Translator's note: Oberland is the part of the Tyrol located in the Inn valley, between the province of Voralberg and Innsbruck.

[2]   Translator's note: Ausserfern is the region located beyond the Fernpass, towards Bavaria.

Anne Poussard, Université de Caen

THE ATLANTIC ARC: FROM VIRTUALITY TO REALITY?
GEOGRAPHY OF A "PROJECT- AREA"*

A Case Study in Social Geography

This thesis reflects a current trend in research into social geography and aims to highlight changes in the relationship between the spatial dimension and different categories of player (i.e. institutional, political, socio-economic and socio-occupational). The thesis uses the example of the Atlantic Arc to identify what some people call "new types of territorial behaviour", or new relationships between the spatial and the social dimension. The Atlantic Arc is therefore an "experimental area"; by analysing the way in which it emerged and took shape, we can understand the relationships between the people involved in public spatial planning and regional development policies, and a reference area (i.e. the Atlantic facade) in terms of a specific area for representation and action (i.e. the Atlantic Arc). The Atlantic Arc is in turn a pretext, study aid and point of entry into this issue, a case-study designed to help us understand the wider issue, rather than a subject of research in itself. Defined as an area whose institutional and conceptual boundaries are still emerging and evolving, the Atlantic Arc stretches the length of the Atlantic coast and was one of the European Union's eight areas of inter-regional cooperation in the early 1990s. This study therefore focuses on the raison d'être of the Atlantic Arc - i.e. an association of local and regional authorities that develop trans-national policies of inter-regional cooperation - rather than on its feasibility.

Firstly, the Atlantic Arc is both the reflection and result of a simultaneous and ongoing period of change, and proof that institutional players and economic decision-makers are adapting to the social, economic and political context. In the absence of a model for interpretation, we decided to analyse the Atlantic Arc by looking at its early phases in terms of the context in which it emerged. We therefore used both a historical and chronological approach to recreate and write the history - though short - of this movement in order to define (i) its progress from virtuality to reality and (ii) its various phases, from the initial political idea of the original association - i.e. the

---

*   Geography thesis, submitted at the University of Caen, 27 September 1997.

Conference of Peripheral Maritime Regions (CPMR) - to the final concept of "project area". Our aim was to identify the factors behind the formal creation of the Atlantic Arc by referring to work which had been carried out in other social science-related fields - e.g. the economy, sociology of organisations, political sciences, etc. - and on several different geographical levels, from local to international. On the basis of these theoretical and methodological frameworks, the thesis focuses on three main areas and uses three different - and complementary - approaches.

Three issues, three multidisciplinary and complementary approaches

Part one reviews the area of inter-regional cooperation covered by Atlantic Arc association members. What borders and geographical realities are behind the invention of the Atlantic Arc idea, or the "Atlantic project area"?

Which criteria other than the associative and political nature of the Atlantic Arc reinforce this area of inter-regional and trans-national cooperation?

Part two looks at the Atlantic Arc in the context in which it emerged, in particular the social, economic and political changes of the past two decades. The thesis looks at the decisive factors in the creation of this project of inter-regional cooperation on various different levels and thereby offers insights, from local to international level, from local and regional authorities to European decision-making bodies (in several fields), and from the economy to the sociology of organisations. The final part considers two different phases. It first suggests how we should interpret the emergence and creation of the Atlantic dynamic and then lists the players, organisations and actions that began to make the Atlantic Arc a reality, six years after it was officially created. Based on field observations, the assessment demonstrates - among other things - the roles and status of the political players and economic decision-makers who helped promote this "project area".

These three very different but complementary approaches are used to explain the emergence of the Atlantic Arc and interpret the implications of setting up such an association of local and regional authorities, who announced their intention to create an area of inter-regional cooperation the length of the European Union's Atlantic facade as long ago as 1989.

Of course, such groupings of local and regional authorities are not a new or unique phenomenon in Western Europe. However, although such associations - which, in fact, shape project areas - have been growing in number for several years, no-one really knew how to synthesise or even identify the motivating factors or creative processes behind such associations of inter-regional cooperation, or their implications for the shape of the European Union.

Two underlying questions constantly informed this analysis throughout the years spent observing and studying the Atlantic dynamic: Is the Atlantic Arc the result of European integration and the advanced phases of the Member States' decentralisation policy? And/or is it not itself part of European integration? Regardless of the answer, the fact that such project areas are being created or invented demonstrates that new relationships are emerging between the people involved in European integration and the ever-closer economic and political area that is the European Union.

THE ATLANTIC ARC OR EXPERIMENTS IN COMMUNITY REGIONAL POLICY

We believe that studying and analysing these relationships to the spatial dimension is vital to understanding and interpreting the Atlantic Arc. Indeed, it soon became clear that such relationships were essential to the emergence of this movement and to the motivation of its founders and, quite simply, as criteria for identifying the area covered by the regions belonging to the Atlantic Arc Commission in relation to other areas of the EU. The reason for this could be that Europe often appears as an imposed idea which, despite being somewhat distant in its projects, has very real political, economic, social and cultural repercussions. Or that Europe, that "vague political, economic and social entity", is above all the result of the activities of human beings who invest, produce and move around in it everyday. These movements within and relationships with the Community area demonstrate new types of territorial behaviour and this in turn calls for new regulatory frameworks and rules. The European Union today is simply the result of these changes.

Like the European Union, the Atlantic Arc has become the subject of opinions, controversies, predictions and speculation. Researchers from various disciplines who became interested in the Atlantic Arc, as well as the very wide-range of people involved in the Atlantic project, talk about new types of territorial behaviour, new models of economic development, new behaviour by local and regional political and economic leaders in response to ever-faster European integration or, finally, an "Atlantic renewal". The latter was considered necessary by some if so-called marginalised areas - or areas heading for marginalisation - were to be integrated into Europe, as if people living along the Atlantic facade were not involved in the great Europe-building project of the end of the 20th century. Again, whichever point of view is chosen, the Atlantic Arc remains a highly-disputed and contentious issue, just as Europe and Maastricht were in the past.

These conflicting opinions nonetheless reveal that experimentation, or rather participation, in European integration has been on the increase for several decades. In response to the rhetoric of crises - e.g. the crisis of the welfare state, the crisis of the governability of democracies, the crisis of citizenship, the crisis of representation, the crisis of the nation state, the crisis of society, the crisis of the economy[1] - people invent different models, patterns of production and projects. The Atlantic project area makes these ambitions a reality and also foreshadows the Europe of tomorrow with slogans such as "Atlantic Arc meetings: Twenty-three European regions echo your plans, welcome to the Atlantic Arc", or "Twenty-three regions are now revitalising trade to bring about change. Europe is being built here, in the Atlantic Arc.".

So, why the Atlantic Arc? Why "Atlantic project area"? Maybe because, in the words of Jean-Pierre Raffarin, "European regions now have such power that one can work with Bilbao, Lisbon or Glasgow without having to go via Paris"[2]. Such discourse, whether by politicians or the media, reflects both real and merely predicted changes and therefore puts the Atlantic Arc back in the context in which it emerged. Although spatial organisation maps were a motivating factor behind the Atlantic movement, they also represented the European political and economic area, including the Atlantic Arc, in a way which contradicted the actual facts.

We therefore took a step back from the Atlantic Arc and tried to look at it from the perspective of the major ideological and conceptual standpoints of the day. From local to global level, from decentralised region to a Europe of Regions, from bottom-up development to top-down development, we combined the thinking and models that

---

[1]   Jobert B., Dir., (1994), Le tournant néo-libéral en Europe. Paris, L'Harmattan, Col. Logiques politiques.
[2]   "Arc Atlantique et équilibre européen", Interview with Jean-Pierre Raffarin, "La réalité régionale et la construction européenne", Inter-régions Magazine, n° 114, 1990.

had been current in Europe, and in particular France, for several decades prior to the creation of the Atlantic Arc. As a result, our interpretation of the context in which the Atlantic Arc emerged looks at the economic, political and institutional levels. This helped us explain and interpret the implications of this project of inter-regional cooperation.

Again, however, there were a few more necessary twists in our journey from virtuality to reality if we were to analyse the Atlantic Arc's spatial and temporal phases from an empirical point of view - i.e. from protest to mobilisation, from the political idea to accession, from accession to organisation and, finally, from organisation to conceptualisation. This was one way of interpreting the Atlantic movement: identifying and interpreting the key phases in the creation of the project area, which could then be applied to other movements. By doing this, we were able to clarify what is hidden beneath the Atlantic dynamic and define the moving forces behind and foundations of the Atlantic Arc in terms of the trends, thinking and models that defined the context in which it emerged.

The changing relationship between the spatial dimension and different categories of player

The next issue for discussion was how the Atlantic project area was created and how programmes of inter-regional cooperation were implemented. Six years of experience show that the Atlantic Arc has real economic consequences for Atlantic regions and that development today needs to take account of a this new dimension. As local and regional authorities become part of larger geographical and economic areas, the spatial dimension is an increasingly important element of economic development. It is perhaps here that the territoriality of the political players becomes one of the keys to development today or, at least, one of the motivating forces behind the emergence of such trans-national projects.

Finally, despite the reservations expressed throughout our interpretation of this Atlantic movement, which is relatively young in the history of European integration, we must also mention the changing relationship between the spatial dimension, on the one hand, and economic players and elected local and regional representatives, on the other. Less than ten years after decentralisation laws shifted powers to local and regional authorities in France, the elected representatives of these new political institutions implemented a policy of Atlantic inter-regional cooperation and began playing the trans-nationality game. Firm believers in local and regional development, they support, encourage and defend trans-national projects, invent project areas and form structures, at other levels, that share this desire to cooperate and thereby increase trade. Both local and regional levels are adopting new approaches to spatial planning and regional development based on new concepts to describe people's changing relationship to the spatial dimension.

Though already old, the concept of a Europe of the Regions has become the pivot of the Atlantic Arc. Other project areas, such as the Southern Europe-Atlantic area and Cross-Channel area, also favour this political concept of the European Union. As well as being innovative and experimental, the Atlantic Arc uses trans-national programmes of inter-regional cooperation to promote forms of spatial planning and economic development that go beyond the national level and are based instead on an intermediate level somewhere between the supranational level and intra-national level, i.e. between local and regional authorities (regions, autonomous regions, counties, etc.) and the area of political and economic integration that is the European Union.

1998/1999

FIGHTING ECONOMIC AND SOCIAL DISPARITIES IN EUROPE: HOW CAN REGIONS AND CITIES CONTRIBUTE TO A MORE BALANCED EU?

Chairman of the jury

Prof. Emilio del Río Sanz (ES), Secretary-General for EU affairs and action outside La Rioja, government of La Rioja

Theses submitted

NUMBER OF ENTRANTS	LANGUAGES		COUNTRY	
25	5	German English Spanish French Italian	9	Germany Austria Spain Finland France Italy Luxembourg Netherlands Sweden

Winners

First prize:

Dr Anne-Sophie Tombeil (DE), *Differing development profiles in Southern Europe. A comparative analysis of the socio-economic processes involved in closing the development gap in certain regions of Italy and Spain*, Faculty of Social and Behavioural Sciences, Tübingen University

Second prize:

Dr Isabelle Trinquelle (FR), *The interplay of region, state and EU in waste management. What role for Europe's regions? Examples from Germany, Belgium, Spain, France and Italy*, University of Paris XI

Special mention:

Dr José Miranda Bonilla (ES), *Community regional policy and its impact in Andalusia*, Faculty of Geography, University of Seville

Anne-Sophie Tombeil, University of Tübingen

Regional development processes in southern Europe - A comparison between the situation in Italy and Spain

Even at the beginning of the 21st century, economic and social disparities between highly-industrialised urban conurbations, on the one hand, and peripheral areas suffering from structural and economic weaknesses, on the other hand, constitute one of the most serious sources of economic, social and political problems for both national states and a European Union which is growing ever closer. Against this background the present study entitled "Regional development processes in southern Europe - A comparison between the situation in Italy and Spain" seeks to shed light on the different approaches adopted by two less-favoured regions in Italy and Spain to the process of catching up with other areas in socio-economic terms. This study poses the following question: Why was regional development in the 1980s and 1990s more successful in Valencia than it was in Calabria? Detailed empirical study of two selected cases which may be regarded, in their respective national contexts, as models of successful and unsuccessful regional development respectively, identifies economic, social and political factors behind the different development profiles of the two less-favoured regions. A two-stage explanation model is formulated in the study. The key element of this model is the breaking down of discrepancies in regional development into a *socio-economic dimension* and an *action* dimension in respect of political action and action by civil society bodies. The socio-economic dimension of regional development relates to the concrete factors applying in the case of the two regions in question and the way in which they developed over the reference period. The action dimension addresses the work carried out by civil society bodies and the structure, processes and content of national, regional and EU policy. What links these two dimensions of regional development is the actual policy-making process. The link between the two dimensions is brought about by the fact that the policies formulated in the light of particular social and political conditions and within the framework of specific political structures and processes, together with the practical implementation of these policies; have a positive or negative impact on the concrete factors which apply in a given region and the development of these factors, thereby determining the way in which the socio-economic catching-up processes is carried out.

The analysis of regional development in the two selected cases pinpoints three key, interdependent factors which may explain the success or failure of the socio-economic catching-up processes employed in the case of the respective regions. The first of these factors is "historical differences"; the second factor is "the attendant economic, social and political conditions" and the third factor is "the management and shaping of these conditions by the respective national and regional authorities and the EU authorities".

The history of the founding of Italy and Spain as national states, together with the historical development of the two countries themselves and the development of the regions under consideration in their national contexts up to the present day, provide the basis for the establishment of a variety of economic, social and political conditions and therefore constitute a key element in explaining the different development profiles.

Turning to Italy, first of all, the Mezzogiorno (south of Italy) in general, which is characterised by an agricultural system based on "latifundia" (large estates) and archaic social patterns, and Calabria, in particular, which is one of the least-favoured regions of the south of Italy, both found themselves in an unfavourable position, right from the time of the establishment of the national state of Italy, vis-à-vis the situation applying in the secular and industrialised north of the country. National reunification was tantamount to a formal act of legal and political annexation of the south by the rest of Italy and did not go hand in hand with an economic and social integration of the two disparate parts of the country. The north-south dichotomy which was already in evidence at this time has continued to the present day.

A characteristic feature of the disparate regional development in Italy is the historically-based, ongoing concentration of economic power and cultural and political hegemony in the north of the country. Overall economic development in Italy was initially driven by the north of Italy alone and subsequently also by central Italy. The regions of southern Italy, for their part, have neither marked regional identities nor home-grown political elites and were unable to develop independent socio-economic structures. The votes of those living in the south of Italy have, however, always been of decisive importance in determining which of the governing parties retains power in Rome. As a result of this set of circumstances, a particular form of political and economic relations has developed between the backward regions of the south and the rest of Italy. General economic policy measures were tailored to meet the requirements of the regions which already enjoyed a favourable status and were continuously adjusted to meet these requirements. Regional policy, on the other hand, was regarded as purely a southern Italian policy which, following an initial period of boom in the 1950s an early 1960s, in which the most serious structural shortcomings were put right and a minimum of state input was provided, degenerated into nothing more than a system for making transfer payments for welfare and social security purposes.

In Italy political action, in general, and action in the field of regional policy, in particular, is not founded on a sense of collective responsibility for joint projects involving overall social and economic development but is rather geared to an exchange - based on patronage - of state-directed resources for political consensus. Bearing in mind that the position of the south of Italy in this exchange system, by virtue of its very backwardness, served the economic and political interests of the already well-favoured regions of Italy, the removal of regional disparities would not work to the benefit of the elite who enjoyed economic and political power. State resources were therefore not used to promote self-supporting development in the less-favoured regions but rather to safeguard social harmony and political and economic power by satisfying the interests of individuals. As a result of this policy, the dichotomy between a highly-industrialised and integrated north of Italy and a marginalised, subsidised south of Italy was reinforced.

In the case of Spain, on the other hand, the foundation of the national state brought together two independent kingdoms which, in their turn, comprised a series of more or less autonomous territories and regions having their own history and culture. The establishment of a new territorial unit, originally called "Las Españas" initially ushered in a territorial and religious fusion but not a political fusion. The key feature of the new political system was the linking of the highest possible level of centralisation, on the one hand, with the recognition of the traditional systems of regional government and regional rights of the former kingdom of Valencia, on the other hand.

A distinguishing feature of the disparate level of regional development in Spain has been the fact that economic power has continuously ebbed and flowed between the various parts of the country and was, moreover, not linked to centralised political power right up until the late 1970s. Against this background and in the light of the moves towards European integration, on the one hand, and the parallel moves towards increasing regional autonomy vis-à-vis central government, on the other hand, the maintenance and expansion of an integrated economic area, enjoying a more or less evenly-balanced level of development, became a vital prerequisite for the establishment of a strong pluralistic state. The removal of regional discrepancies in Spain is a matter of vital interest for the country as a whole and its component parts. Measures to promote regional development are therefore an integral part of overall economic policy. The shared goal of modernising the Spanish economy to bring it into line with the rest of the EU and to make it competitive on the world market, with a view to promoting overall economic growth, lies at the heart of economic and regional policy. Economic and regional policy funding, at both national and regional level, is focussed on the achievement of this goal. Funding provided by the EU has up to now been seen as a necessary and welcome additional source of funding which has been fully integrated into national and regional budgets and used to promote the achievement of the above goals. By pursuing this policy it has been possible to achieve a remarkable level of aggregate growth which has also had a beneficial effect on the less-favoured regions.

The Autonomous Community of Valencia has been able to establish independent socio-economic structures from the outset for a number of reasons: the historical reason, linked to Valencia's earlier experience of self-determination and autonomy; its strong regional identity and its open-minded regional population; the geographical advantages it enjoys as a result of proximity to the sea; and finally its Mediterranean climate. The establishment of these independent socio-economic structures was clearly a key prerequisite for the dynamic development of the Valencia region in the second half of the 20th century. A number of factors have brought and continue to bring clear advantages to the Valencia region, namely: the functionally-integrated, poly-nuclear urban structure; the high level of economic cohesion in long-established industrial districts, based on craft industries and subsequently on industrial production; and a dynamic trade and sectoral structure based on deeply-rooted craft traditions and specific expertise in the region. Mention should also be made of a number of further important prerequisites for successful autonomous and self-sustaining development, such as: the existence of independent entrepreneurs; traditional links with external markets; a complex pattern of reciprocal trade, and a deep-seated belief in regional identity, culture and dynamism, which are characteristic features of regional civil society. Turning to the political field, the predominance of strong, convergent governments at both national and regional level (which have demonstrated stability over several terms of office), backed up by political consensus between broad categories of the population over basic economic policy and policy towards Europe, have been highly conducive to a coherent management and organisation of long-term socio-economic development processes. Finally, the fact that administrative action at both national and regional level was brought into line at an early stage with the structures - but not the content - of EU regional policy facilitated the exploitation and effective use of EU funding to promote the national and regional development strategy.

This comparatively favourable initial situation in Valencia led to the harnessing, organisation and revitalisation of the socio-economic potential of the region. National and regional-level political bodies showed themselves to be effective players here in organising and directing regional development through the establishment of the necessary overall conditions and the promotion of modernisation and synergy. By way of example, attention is drawn to the efforts to develop transport infrastructure and telecommunications, making full use of resources provided by the European Structural Funds (to which the European Commission was initially opposed) and the establishment of efficient network-type structures, such as the IMPIVA and similar institutes, to provide dedicated support for production structures in the Valencia region. Regional political bodies in the Valencia region have proved to be particularly effective in managing and organising the socio-economic catching-up processes during the reference period. The strategy which has been pursued - and in part already implemented - is based on the promotion of endogenous development as a specific means of adapting, modernising and expanding the available production infrastructure. This approach facilitated optimal exploitation of local resources and the promotion of socio-economic development in the region, without cutting the links with its traditional roots. Despite the fact that the autonomy, as regards decision-making and action, of the Autonomous Communities in Spain is limited by the dominance of national political bodies in respect of all decisive fundamental issues, the example of Valencia demonstrates that regional political bodies can make a decisive contribution to the management and organisation of socio-economic catching-up processes in their own regions by exploiting the available room for manoeuvre and resources in order to establish conditions which promote independent development.

In contrast to Valencia, Calabria has a history marked by foreign rule, subjugation and exploitation, compounded by a period of feudalism which extended, almost without interruption, into the 1950s. The development of a self-assured, independent and cooperative civil society was, to a large extent, prevented by a number of factors: the predominance of an individualistic attitude marked by self-interest amongst the key players; and a deep distrust of the state and its institutions on the part of the regional population of Calabria (compounded by the pervasion of society by a political system based on patronage and "back-scratching"). Despite the fact that Calabria and Valencia enjoy similar favourable geographic and climatic conditions, Calabria was unable to establish independent socio-economic structures. Structural disadvantages deriving from historical factors have so far posed enormous impediments to regional development in Calabria. Examples of these disadvantages are: a fragmented and dispersed settlement structure; the lack of economic agglomeration and cooperation; and unfavourable industrial and sectoral structures, characterised by a wholly marginal manufacturing sector and a huge, well-funded service sector. The problem is further aggravated by the lack of a tradition of entrepreneurial own-account working in the craft, industrial and service sectors; the predominance of economic organisation characterised by hand-outs and parasitic behaviour; and the problem of organised crime.

At both national and regional level the formulation and implementation of consistent, longer-term development policies have been rendered impossible by the marked weakness of governments which have not only been constantly changing but which have also lacked congruence; the problem has been exacerbated by the lack of a will to give political priority to the removal of regional disparities. In Italy regional-policy measures were not seen as key components of general economic policy and incorporated into this policy; regional policy measures were rather always introduced when changes in the economic situation made it necessary to safeguard the viability of the less-favoured regions in order to protect the overall system. There is a sharp discrepancy between the policies which are formulated and their actual implementation because of a number of factors; complex bureaucratic procedures; cumbersome administrative machinery; and, especially, the lack of a political will to make a real effort to promote autonomous development in the south of Italy. The goals set continue to be abstract and have led to very few concrete projects designed to meet the specific needs of the region. Successful efforts have, however, been made to improve the standard of living and raise the level of consumption in the south of

Italy by means of a policy of transferring resources to the south on welfare grounds. Little attempt has, however, been made to pursue and implement concrete political measures to overcome structural weaknesses, bring about more effective exploitation of the endogenous potential which is also available in Calabria and to increase the level of socio-economic competitiveness of the region. Furthermore, a number of factors have conspired to make it more difficult to match the work of administrative bodies with the conditions for receiving aid under the European Structural Funds, with the result that it has up to now scarcely been possible to use funding from this source, too, to remove regional disparities. The factors involved here are the lack of institutional flexibility, the decrepit structures and the fixed allocation arrangements under the national system of regional aid which has been in existence for decades. Calabria has up to now been pathologically dependent on external funding. The regional government has so far been unable to make use of the available funding and opportunities for managing and organising socio-economic catching-up processes in the region and thereby setting in train an autonomous development process.

To sum up, the initial finding of this analysis is that there is a direct link between the nature of the primary inputs, economic structure and the labour supply structure, on the one hand, and the socio-economic catching-up processes pursued in a given region, on the other hand. The higher level of regional development in Valencia can thus be explained by the fact that this region has more favourable socio-economic structural variables. The analysis has also shown that the remarkably high level of development in Valencia can not be put down solely to the more favourable initial situation as regards the key socio-economic structural variables; it has been achieved rather through the exploitation and reinvigoration of the existing structures by an energetic, open and adaptable civil society which has evolved over a long period of time. Success has been achieved, in particular, through political management and organisation by a capable political elite operating at national, and in particular, regional level. This positive political achievement was in turn facilitated by the network-structure pertaining in regional development in both Spain and Valencia. As regards policy-formulation at national and regional level, and in particular, as regards the implementation of the development-policy measures in the region, this network structure is characterised by a broad horizontally-integrated organisation resembling a political alliance. This structure is backed up by interaction and decision-making processes through which medium or longer-term coherent strategies are formulated and implemented by national political bodies, adopting a proactive approach to dealing with the problems involved. Strategies are either formulated on a consensual basis or, where necessary, a firmer and more assertive line may be adopted.

The stagnation and growing marginalisation of Calabria may thus be explained by the comparatively unfavourable socio-economic factors which prevail, and in particular, by the fact that neither the national nor the regional administrations have so far pursued and implemented political measures capable of improving the socio-economic structural variables and bringing about more effective exploitation of the endogenous potential. This political failure can in turn be put down to the specific network structure and the political style adopted in Italy which is characterised by relations based on patronage and a tendency to drift and muddle through when decisions are to be taken. Politics amounts to little more than short-term, ad hoc, reactive, crisis-management measures of little substance when it comes to providing solutions.

The second finding of this study is that the two-stage model developed in the study has proved to be of considerable value in providing explanations for the cases which have been examined. Breaking the overall phenomenon of discrepancies in regional development down into a socio-economic dimension and a dimension covering action by civil society and political bodies has proved to be a good approach. A detailed analysis of these two dimensions pinpointed the socio-economic political-institutional and political and process-related factors behind the policies and policy outcomes which determine regional development in Calabria and Valencia. The key importance of political management and organisation in providing an explanation for differences in the level of success of development measures has been demonstrated. Empirical case studies show that socio-economic structural variables represent an important prerequisite for and, so to speak, determine the scope of development in a given regional economic area. A decisive element in determining the success of socio-economic catching-up processes is, however, the development of factors of production through the organisation and exploitation of the existing resources - including resources from the European Structural Funds - by social and political bodies in the states and regions concerned. With this aim in view appropriate policies need to be formulated and implemented.

A third finding of this study is that, in both of the cases which have been examined, it has been shown that European regional policy is far more dependent upon national and regional political structures and processes and has much less influence on the shaping of these structures and processes than has frequently been acknowledged. The rapid implementation of key development policy measures in Spain can thus be attributed to the fact that the national players did **not**, at least in the initial round of providing aid, align their policy on the detailed objectives of EU regional policy but, rather, single-mindedly pursued and implemented their own objectives. In Calabria, on the other hand, both at national and at regional level, regional-policy objectives were not implemented consistently, EU aid policy was out of step with regional requirements and possibilities in many areas; and available funding could not be used. The development of precisely the most needy regions is therefore being hindered rather than promoted by the over-ambitious EU objectives and provisions.

The fourth finding of the study is that empirical investigation of the two selected cases shows no clear preference for any one of the three basic types of explanation models in respect of differences in regional development and the consequent recommendations for action, which emerged from the theoretical debate. The example of Valencia did indeed demonstrate that (a) explanation models based on endogenous factors involving territory, participation and cooperation, (b) the recommendation that action be taken to promote economic, political and social networking and (c) the appreciation and exploitation of endogenous potential all apply to this specific region. A further recommended objective - extensive decentralisation of political decision-making power and the comprehensive participation of economic, political and social forces - is not, however, being implemented in Spain. On the contrary, the national political level is the dominant player in determining general economic policy, of which regional policy is a component part. Success in the field of development policy in Spain is so far largely attributable to centralised planning and programming. This form of state control does not however clearly fit in with the standard Keynesian or polarisation-theory explanation model since, during the period covered by the study, whilst the PSOE Government reserved the right to engage in state control of key political areas, it did however, at the same time endeavour achieve market expansion through deregulation and liberalisation measures. Furthermore, the sub-national political level in Spain is continually gaining further scope for action and making an ever greater contribution to the shaping of regional economic areas. The example of Calabria shows that in the case of markedly lagging regions which do not have either the necessary structures or adequate powers for managing and organising socio-economic catching-up processes, endogenous strategies do not constitute a fair alternative in developed states but rather constitute an "opt-out" of responsibility on the part of national political bodies. In the case of Calabria there is clearly a need to create, by means of targeted, committed national policy, the structural prerequisites, first of all, and subsequently also the social and political prerequisites for autonomous development before primary responsibility can be handed over to the regional level. The example of Italy also shows that neo-classical types of explanation models and their concepts of balance, harmony and the market have no relevance whatsoever in states characterised by marked regional disparities.

The cases which have been examined in this study demonstrate that the Spanish policy based on (a) the dominant objective of overall economic growth and (b) central government providing the link between development policy measures organised at regional level has successfully managed to achieve a balance between a coordinating, hierarchical centralisation, on the one hand, and flexible, grass-roots level, innovative decentralisation, on the other hand. Integration of national economic policy and regional policy with the aim of pursuing the common objective of overall economic growth, as a means of promoting national and European integration, has proved to be a more effective form of organisation than the separation of national economic policy - which in Italy in reality only took account of the interests of the developed part of the country - from regional policy and the establishment of a specific policy for the south of Italy, which amounted to nothing more than the transfer of funding for charitable and welfare reasons. It has been demonstrated that regional disparities can be removed if regional policy becomes an integral part of a general economic policy which encompasses the whole of the national economic area and promotes the effectiveness of the overall system.

It is now clear that, even two years after its conclusion, the findings of this study have not lost their relevance. On the contrary, attention is drawn to the fact that two of the points empirically demonstrated in this study form part of the current debate on ways of strengthening economic and social cohesion in the EU, also with a view to the accession of the central and eastern European countries. The points in question are: the effectiveness of integrated approaches in respect of both the objectives of regional policy measures and as regards the players involved in formulating and implementing policy; and the importance of the civil-society forces.

Following its success in improving the provision at regional level of productive capital and transport infrastructure, in the new aid round Spain has set itself the objective of extending its regional policy strategy to include the enhancement of regional production infrastructure and increasing investment activity and capacity for innovation in the regions (cf. the Community aid blueprint for the Spanish Objective 1 Regions - 2000-2006). In the case of Italy (cf. the Community aid blueprint for the Italian Objective 1 Regions - 2000-2006), whilst there have been no major successes in removing the disparities between the north and south of the country, greater political stability and the reform of regional electoral law sent out positive signals for strengthening of both civil society and economic growth. Attention is also drawn in this context to the improvement in state inputs and services and the stemming of organised crime. All of this progress helps to enhance the public confidence in the state's ability to ensure the security of, for example, investment and economic activity.

The Sixth Periodic Report on the Socio-economic Situation and Development of the Regions (1999) expressly referred to the complexity of regional development processes and the attendant need to take appropriate account of the interplay between the different factors (page 9). The importance of "social capital" is also highlighted in the report, which defines it in terms of elements such as entrepreneurial spirit, administrative structures and institutional relations; this terms corresponds directly with the term "civil society forces" used in the study under review to define a factor in the action dimension of regional development.

In general, it may be stated that the procedural model formulated in the present study provides an appropriate framework for analysing and assessing regional development processes. The study makes it possible to identify the factors determining regional development and thus assist regional-development players and institutions involved in regional development in the pursuit of their goal of establishing a "learning organisation" (see page 10 et seq of the Sixth Periodical Report).

A detailed bibliography is set out in the book version of the Study on Regional Development Processes in southern Europe - A comparison between the situation in Italy and Spain, Wiesbaden 1999, ISBN 3 - 8244-4362-7

States. The role of the regions of Europe[3] in the implementation of this common policy has therefore been affirmed. At first sight, the responsibilities for regional planning, which are traditionally devolved to the regional authorities, should enable them to take part in the management of such a sector, which is connected with the economy, the environment and social affairs. However, the intervention of the regions inevitably raises the question of the compatibility between a common policy and diversified application.

I.   The potential of the regions in the implementation of the European waste management strategy

The distribution of responsibilities for waste management shows two major trends: Member States have transferred most of the relevant legal measures to the Community authorities, while in several Member States the regions have been given increased responsibility for implementing policy.

A.   Sustainable waste management and a territorial approach

1.   A European strategy linked to the territorial context

Initially, Community intervention as regards waste was aimed primarily at anticipating the possible impact on the Common Market of the measures taken individually by the Member States. European legislation therefore first attempted to define a common framework of rules[4] and to regulate well identified problems through a series of directives[5]. Then, after the Single European Act had confirmed and legitimised the Community's jurisdiction as regards the environment by introducing Articles 130 R to S (now Articles 174 to 176) into the Treaty, the European

---

[3]   The region is here understood to mean the sub-national authority closest to the national level. We will mention the French, Italian and Belgian regions, the Spanish autonomous communities, and the German *Länder*.

[4]   Directive 75/442/EEC of 15 July 1975 concerning waste (OJ L194 1975 p.39).

[5]   For example: Directive 75/439/EEC of 16 June 1975 on the elimination of waste oils (OJ L194 1975 p.23) or Directive 78/176/EEC of 20 February 1978 on waste from the titanium dioxide industry (OJ L54 1978 p.19).

Community beefed up its policy by formulating a European waste management strategy[6] which established three top priorities arranged in the following order:

- limit waste production;
- make better use of the matter and, in the second place, the energy produced;
- dispose of unavoidable waste under the best possible conditions for health and the environment.

To these guidelines, which comply with the principles of prevention and the management at source of environmental concerns (Article 174 of the Treaty), are added the limitation and monitoring of transfers of waste from one state to another. Priority has to be given to disposing of waste as close as possible to the place where it is produced (the principle of proximity), which involves increasing elimination capacities in each Member State and within the Union as a whole (the principle of self-sufficiency) [7].

However, more than 20 years after the first directive on the matter, because of the close link between economic growth and the generation of waste, improvements in processing have not succeeded in slowing the increase in the overall volume of waste[8]. To counteract this tendency, European policy is directed towards improving the prevention of waste production through an integrated approach[9]. This means that the question of waste has to be taken into account in all other policies (relating to goods, energy, transport etc.)[10]. Such an approach is therefore closely linked to the specific context of each territory (main types of activity, consumers' behaviour and habits, waste processing capacity, market organisation, etc.).

---

[6]   Community strategy for waste management (Communication from the EC Commission to the Council and Parliament of 14 September 1989, SEC(89) 934 final) and its review (Communication from the EC Commission to the Council and Parliament, COM(96) 399 final).

[7]   See Article 5 of Directive 75/442/EEC as amended by Directive 91/156/EEC. In order not to restrict the possibilities for upgrading waste, these two principles only apply to waste elimination.

[8]   See Environment in the European Union at the turn of the century - Environmental Assessment Report no. 2 - European Environment Agency 1999, p. 203 et seq.

[9]   See in particular the 6th Community action programme on 2001-2010 environment "2010 Environment: our future, our choice" COM(2001) 31.

[10]   Article 6 of the Treaty: "Environmental protection requirements must be integrated into the definition and implementation of other policies".

Management at source, proximity, self-sufficiency, integration ..., Community principles lie at the root of waste management on the ground and justify a regional approach to the waste issue. But in the face of these common ambitions, the regions encounter various difficulties depending on several factors.

In practice, the dominant sector of activity in a given region determines the types of waste and the inherent constraints: liquid manure from pig farms in Brittany and its problems of water pollution, tourist activity in coastal regions and its major variations in waste flows involving either an oversizing of facilities or chronic deficiencies in processing capacity, etc. Some regions, late developers, are lacking in adequate infrastructure and specialist human resources, and do not manage to satisfy the requirements of European regulations. The geographical context can also come into play: the most remote regions, like certain island regions, not only lack equipment but are also a long way away from the continental mainland. As they are forced to transfer waste over long distances, they have to bear excessive management costs and violate the principles of proximity and of self-sufficiency.

2.   The role of the regions in implementing common policy

In order to take account of these specific features, regions have fairly wide powers, allowing them a variable degree of involvement in waste management. However, whatever the extent of their legal and material resources, regions have all committed themselves on the ground to waste management.

It is up to the Member States to designate the authorities responsible for implementing the main obligations imposed by the Community[11], which guarantee preventive intervention in the planning of waste management and the follow-up and monitoring of operations to which waste is subjected. All the Member States now have laws concerning waste that transpose more or less correctly the main obligations imposed by European directives. These, coupled with the principles of institutional organisation specific to each state, define the terms of reference of the regional authorities.

To guarantee territorial consistency in the actions carried out as regards waste management, there are many national laws which make the regions responsible for the

---

[11]   Article 6 of Directive 75/442/EEC of 15 July 1975 as amended in 1991 (91/156/EC).

planning of waste management. Even the French regions, despite the lack of powers expressly granted to them, are allowed to take over the drawing-up of the regional plan for the disposal of special industrial waste[12]. The Italian regions[13], the German Länder[14], the Spanish communities[15] and the three Belgian regions are responsible for the planning of waste on their respective territories, and can also co ordinate the actions of other local authorities in this area and ensure the consistency of the actions carried out on their territory.

The possibility of going further, of adapting the general guidelines specified by national framework laws and European directives to a specific context, is reserved for regions with legislative and/or regulatory powers. This possibility is granted in particular to the Spanish autonomous communities[16] and to the German Länder, which hold competing powers on the matter, although national law takes precedence[17]. As for the Belgian regions, they establish themselves the "general and sectoral standards" as regards waste and regulate waste imports and exports as far as the regional territory is concerned[18].

Apart from specific waste management powers, the regions have other means of intervention. Economic measures are among those most used. Financial aid for companies or municipalities can encourage the development of clean technologies, of separate collecting systems or of new facilities. Let us mention Catalonia and its fund to help municipalities manage urban waste[19]; the Walloon Region and its financial support for municipalities ranging from 55 to 85% for the placing of containers for selective collection. Taxation, whose efficacy has been verified[20], is also used by those regions which have the power to do so: the Catalan legislative decree 2/1991 of 26 September 1991 approving the re-casting of the texts on industrial waste was the

---

[12]   Article 10-1 of the Law of 15 July 1975 on waste amended by the Law of 2 February 1995 on the strengthening of environmental protection.

[13]   Article 6 of the DPR 915/1982 on the management of waste and State Law 142/1990 authorising the regions to delegate certain powers to the provinces and Decree-Law n°22 of 5 February 1997.

[14]   Article 6 of the Law of 27 August 1986.

[15]   Article 4 of Law 10/1998 of 21 April on waste.

[16]   Article 149.1.23 of the Constitution and distribution of powers laid down by Law 10/1998 of 21 April.

[17]   Article 74 of the Basic Law. In principle the *Land* can legislate where the federal government has not done so.

[18]   Special law of 16 July 1993 amending the law of 8 August 1980.

[19]   Articles 48 to 51 of Catalonian law 6/1993.

[20]   See the report of the European Environment Agency ("Environmental taxes - Implementation and environmental effectiveness, Environmental issues series n°1, Copenhagen, 1996).

first Spanish legal instrument to provide for specific arrangements for taxing the production of waste production or the products or raw materials contained in it. This tax is intended to help municipalities reduce the impact of industrial waste on the environment. These measures form part of the integrated approach to waste management and encourage the development of joint action.

B.   The limits to regional action

However, the exercising of such powers by the regions poses some problems under Community law. Can the harmonisation sought in the management of environmental problems be consistent with respect for regional diversity?

1.   Regional measures versus uniform application

Regional measures appear initially to be limited by the rules of the market. Measures initiated in the field of waste management have a big impact on the economy: preventive measures are tied to products and to the method used for manufacturing and marketing them; management measures impose specific constraints on producers and on the community (monitoring, sorting, specific equipment, taxes, etc.) which of necessity weigh on their activities. It is in order to avoid the negative impact of these measures on the setting-up and smooth operation of the internal market that the Community is seeking to harmonise the taxes on waste . Since regional "adaptation" measures are unilateral, they breach the harmonised structure and therefore risk being considered as barriers to trade or distortions of competition.

The harmonisation which is sought will also be jeopardised by any provision which allows a region facing particular difficulties extra deadlines beyond those laid down for implementing directives[21].

The aim of standardising the rules on waste is not just to ensure the smooth operation of the market; it is also supposed to guarantee the effectiveness of European environmental law, since the maintenance of differing schemes may reduce the effectiveness of European environmental policy. It is acknowledged that the most lax

---

[21]   For example : CJEC 22 September 1976, aff. 10/76 Commission against Italy, ECR p. 1359; CJEC 24 Nov. 1987, aff. 124/86 Commission against Italy, ECR p.4661; CJEC 24 May 1988 aff. 307/86 Commission against Belgium ECR 2677; CJEC 13 December 1990 aff. C70/89 Commission against Italy, ECR p. I-4821.

of the regulations allow cheap waste disposal and thus encourage methods which are inconsistent with the aims of reducing or upgrading waste (in general placing on rubbish tips)[22]. Similarly, describing an object or a substance as "waste" has major consequences as far as environmental and health protection measures are concerned. The numerous debates on the difference between "waste" and "products" show the difficulties of arriving at a common definition of waste. In Belgium for example, even though the legislation of the Brussels-Capital Region had not drawn up a European Waste Catalogue[23], in July 2000, the Commission sent a reasoned opinion to Belgium because the Walloon Region was incapable of transposing the European definition of waste. How can one expect an identical transposition of the definition of waste and of the obligations surrounding it if each region in a Member State develops its own ideas[24]?

The arsenal of legal measures in force is often so complex as to be ineffective. For instance, when Spanish Autonomous Communities pass legislation on a particular type of waste, sometimes with the aim of affirming the extension of their terms of reference, they inevitably add to "legislative inflation"[25]. The lack of transparency inherent in all this is also an obstacle for the Commission, which does not have the means necessary to carry out its mission of monitoring the application of European texts and identifying and analysing the tangle of domestic provisions implementing European law on waste.

2.   Regional action versus national responsibility

In theory, European law is indifferent about which authority is responsible under domestic law for implementing Community provisions concerning waste (principle of

---

[22]   Cf. Environment in the European Union at the turn of the century - Environmental Assessment Report no. 2 - European Environmental Agency 1999, p.

[23]   Cf. Commission Report on the implementation of Community legislation on waste. COM(1999) 752 final, p. 10.

[24]   The regulations of the Flemish Region and the Walloon Region have led to two separate concepts of dangerous waste. Cf. L. Lavrysen: "La notion de 'déchets' dans la législation existante", Aménagement-Environnement, 1990/n°spécial déchets, p.5-13.

[25]   In occupying the ground left vacant by the central government, which had not adopted specific measures on hospital waste, many of the Autonomous Communities adopted special regulations for this type of waste. Although such intervention by the regions comes within the legal framework laid down by the state, it multiplies the classifications and arrangements applicable to each waste category. See too the example of the Basque Country's initiative as regards regulation of the management of "inert waste".

institutional autonomy). However, the freedom of each Member State to distribute domestic responsibilities "should not exempt it from the obligation to ensure that the provisions of the directive [are] translated accurately into national law"[26]. It is worth remembering here that the European Court has always refused to allow Member States the possibility of justifying failures to apply waste legislation by citing domestic institutional failures[27] or the inaction of the regional authorities[28]. According to the Court, the fact that the failure is noted only on a part of the territory (a single region[29], an island[30]) does not discharge the Member State of its responsibility. But regions are not free from laxism, and the Commission Report on the application of the directives on waste shows up the shortcomings which are as much the fault of the state administration as of the territorial authorities[31].

One is therefore in the somewhat paradoxical situation where regions have wider powers to implement directives on "waste" without being liable directly to the European authorities, while at the same time internal decentralisation and federalism of necessity mean a restriction of the state's means of control over the acts of the regional authorities. This situation has led to a "recentralisation" of the responsibilities for transposing EU directives to the benefit of central government.

II.   Overcoming contradictions to optimise the role of the regions

In spite of these contradictions, several arguments resulting from the Treaty and from secondary legislation are leading to the recognition of regional diversity and the need for a certain room for manoeuvre in the implementation of waste management policy.

---

[26]   CJEC 14 January 1988, aff. Jointes 227 to 230/85, Commission against Belgium, ECR I p. 1.

[27]   For example, CJEC 6 May 1980, aff. 102/79 Commission against Belgium, ECR p.1473; CJEC 18 March 1980 aff. 91/79 Commission against Italy, ECR p. 1099.

[28]   "*any Member State is liable to the Community for any failure by one of its entities to apply Community law*" CJEC 12 January 1994, aff. C 296/92 Commission c/Italy, ECR p. I-1.

[29]   See the case of the Italian State being declared liable for the failure of the Region of Campania, which had not drawn up a waste management plan as required by Article 6 of the outline proposal, or a programme for the disposal of dangerous waste as laid down by Directive 78/318 on toxic and dangerous waste (CJEC 13 December 1991, aff. C33/90 Commission against Italy, ECR I 6001).

[30]   See the case of Greece being condemned by the European Court on the grounds that a part of its territory, in this case Crete, did not have a plan for the elimination of dangerous waste and that no specific elimination of this type of waste was envisaged (CJEC 7 April 1992, aff. 75/91 Commission against Greece, ECR p. I 2509). Greece was obliged to pay a fine for non-implementation of the decision referred to above (cf. CJEC 4 July 2000, C 387/97 Commission v Hellenic Republic).

[31]   Cf. Commission Report on the implementation of Community legislation on waste. COM(1999) 752

A.   Striking a balance between European unity and territorial diversity

1.   Recognising specific regional features

The Community set itself limits on exercising its powers by means of the principles of subsidiarity and proportionality[32]. If these principles are applied, European regulations on waste management are only justified when they are appropriate and in proportion to the objective sought. Given the diversity of the situations that it has to regulate, the Community cannot have a "monopoly of excellence". As the guarantee of optimum waste management does not necessarily rest on measures of Community law, there is still a place for intervention by the authorities of the Member States when they are in a better position to react[33].

Moreover, the economic and social cohesion policy of the European Union recognises the specific nature of regions[34]. It also gives way on environmental matters: environmental policy as defined by the Treaty: *"aims at a high level of protection, bearing in mind the diversity of the situations in the various regions of the Community...". "In the development of its policy in the field of the environment, the Community shall take account [...] of the economic and social development of the Community as a whole and of the balanced development of its regions"* (Article 174, ex-article 130R, paragraph 2 and 3 of the Treaty).

European law on waste recognises the need to respect the specific features of regions by granting certain exemptions. Thus Article 3§4 of the directive on waste disposal provides for a specific application concerning isolated islands and sites which will be designated to the Commission by the Member States. Within these territories, it is

---

[32]   Cf. Article 5 (formerly Article 3B) of the Treaty.

[33]   In its resolution on the application of the principle of subsidiarity to environmental policy, the European Parliament said it wished to "insist that local, regional and national measures which improve the level of protection of Community standards are also protected". European Parliament, A3-0380/92 OJ C42 15/2/93 p. 42.

[34]   Article 158 of the Treaty: "In order to promote harmonious development of the Community, the latter shall develop and continue its actions aimed at strengthening its economic and social cohesion. *In particular, the Community shall aim to reduce the gap between the development levels of the various regions and the backwardness of the least favoured regions or islands, including the rural areas".* Article 299§2 of the Treaty must also be mentioned here since it provides for account to be taken of the particular difficulties of the most remote regions.

possible to be exempted from certain important obligations of the directive[35]. Account has to be taken of the reality on the ground: in the majority of small islands and isolated sites, the existing rubbish tips are unable to fulfil the requirements of European law, although they remain the main destination of household and similar waste[36].

These provisions amount to recognising that *"a unified legal area is not an aim in itself (and that) the principle of subsidiarity ensures diversity in unity"*[37].

2. Strengthening links between the actors

As regards waste management, it is particularly important to make sure that the decisions adopted are the reflection of existing and future needs and capacity. The adoption of measures which are impractical or do not suit the realities on the ground can only lead to their non-implementation. The recognition of diversity has therefore to be accompanied by greater co-operation as regards the development of common rules and their application.

The Community has given itself the institutional means of taking into consideration the diversity of its territory in its environmental policy. The Committee of the Regions gives the regions official representation among the European authorities. It must be consulted on matters involving environmental protection[38]. Moreover, regional authorities of ministerial rank now have access to the Council of Ministers in order to take part directly in EU decision-making in areas which fall exclusively within their

---

[35] Directive 99/31 of 26 April 1999, OJ L182 of 16.7.1999. Exemption will only be possible for rubbish tips intended to hold non-dangerous or inert waste serving these territories : when the site is of a total capacity not exceeding 15,000 tonnes or accepting not more than 1,000 tonnes a year, and when the site is the only rubbish tip on the island and is intended only for the reception of waste produced on the island. Exemptions concern for example : the obligation to receive only inert waste in rubbish tips intended for such (Article 6 d.) or the requirement of a financial guarantee from the operator of a tip (Article 7 i)

[36] See too Article 6§5 of Directive 94/62/EC of the European Parliament and of the Council of 20 December 1994 relating to packaging and the waste from packaging (OJ N° L 365 of 31/12/1994 p. 0010 - 0023) which also takes account of specific territorial features to grant longer deadlines to certain Member States. Beneficiaries may be exempted from the development and recycling targets imposed by the directive.

[37] "Essential subsidiarity and democratic debate, elements of a European legal area" E. Gottfried Mahrenholz, Review of the Common Market and the EU n°438 May 2000, p. 323-324.

[38] Since the changes made by the Treaty of Amsterdam.

jurisdiction (Article 203, ex-Article 146, of the Treaty). The three Belgian regions can thus take part in the drafting of EU texts concerning waste. Moreover, some regions ensure their presence on the European scene either individually or within regroupings[39].

However, the difficulties of arriving at a joint position before the final vote, as well as the additional obstacles that will inevitably arise with the arrival of new Member States, make it difficult to conceive how regional authorities will participate directly in the EU's decision-making process. The environment, like the regions, has certainly more to gain from action by the regions which ensures a better flow of information from the latter's territory to the European authorities. Regional representation must not confine itself to adopting a purely defensive attitude and making demands; it must organises a genuine partnership with the EU institutions. For example, a large region that produces drinks marketed in glass bottles must develop measures to encourage the recycling of glass, rather than seeking to favour its own producers by pushing for draconian measures against other types of packaging.

The implementation of waste management policy is a matter of internal consistency. But the distribution of powers sometimes appears ill-suited to rational waste management: in France, regions may assume responsibility for plans to deal with dangerous industrial waste without having the legal means to implement them (lack of regulatory powers, lack of powers to constrain lower authorities, lack of police powers to authorise or prohibit processing or elimination facilities, or waste imports on to their territory, etc.); in Belgium, since product standards are still a matter for central government, the Belgian regions can do nothing about the origin of waste (composition, manufacture and marketing of products), in spite of their extensive powers in this area; finally, in Germany, the fact that responsibility for waste regulations is shared between central government and the federal states causes conflict, as is shown in the opinion that the Commission sent to Germany in July 2000, which notes the inconsistencies between the definitions of waste adopted by federal and by state legislation.

In the absence of a rationalisation of existing schemes, co-operation must try and offset the fragmentation of responsibilities. But unfortunately this does not happen by

---

[39] See for example, as regards the environment, the FEDARENE which federates regional energy and environmental agencies.

itself; it has to be organised. In Belgium, for example, while waste imports and exports are the responsibility of the regions, the transit of waste remains the responsibility of national legislation. However, the executive of the regions is associated with the state in the preparation of federal standards relating to the transit of waste[40] and a co-operation agreement has enabled the state and the regions to agree on the technical standards for implementing the European Regulation on the transfer of waste[41].

Within the same region, the strengthening of the links between players and policies is also a pledge of integrated management. Thus, the "waste channel" approach (packaging, broken-down vehicles, etc.) promoted by the European strategy in order to better tackle waste limitation at source and get an advance on the possibilities of recycling[42], presupposes an interest in the design, composition and use of the type of product concerned, in existing solutions for the recycling, processing or final elimination of products near their place of production, and in possible outlets for recycled materials. Such a step assumes the participation of all the actors in a sector of activity on the territory concerned. The regional advantage then becomes apparent because the regions have this facility of covering an area that is sufficiently broad to include all the actors likely to be involved in the management of most of the categories of waste and sufficiently restricted to facilitate the setting-up of a complete and coherent channel. They must not fail in their role of territorial co-ordinator. European co-funding of regional programmes can help this approach provided that it is really directed towards projects that fulfil environmental requirements and are managed by the regional authorities themselves.

Finally, a link must be established between the regions themselves in order to encourage a territorial approach that is not determined by inoperable administrative boundaries. Certain categories of dangerous waste in particular can be produced in quantities that are too small to make an on-the-spot disposal plant viable. Efforts then

---

[40]   Article 6 §4 1° of the special law of 8 August 1980 amended by the special law of 16 July 1993.

[41]   Cf. Co-operation agreement between the Belgian state, the Flemish Region, the Walloon Region and the Region of Brussels-capital on the co-ordination of policy on the import, export and transit of waste, signed on 26.10.1994.

[42]   Programme launched by the European Union in 1990 for a Community action as regards priority waste flows. Cf. the Council Resolution of 7 May 1990 90/C 112/02 of the Council on policy regarding waste (OJ C 122 of 18 May 1990 p. 2); Commission Report to the Council and Parliament on waste management, 8 November 1995, COM(92) 522 final, p.11 et seq.

should be geared to a plant able to handle waste produced in small quantities on several adjoining territories. It could be easier to reach the critical mass needed to guarantee the plant's profitability[43]. Authorities will therefore find it is in their interest to co-ordinate their activities right from the stage of drawing up their waste management plans, in order to achieve a territorial consistency that is both economic and ecological.

B.   Striking a balance between protecting the rules of the market and protecting the environment

1.   Waivers from uniform application

It is, as a matter of principle, inconceivable that harmonising standards could take precedence over guaranteeing a higher level of environmental protection. Community law therefore recognises, in exceptional circumstances, the possibility of adopting specific measures that differ from the rules of the market when environmental protection so requires[44]. Moreover, domestic authorities may adopt or maintain stricter provisions than those laid down in European directives concerning the environment[45].

These exceptions to the common rules are nevertheless limited and checked by the Commission. Domestic measures will only be considered legitimate from the point of view of Community law if, on the one hand, they are in keeping with the aim of

---

[43]   Article 4§3 a) ii of Regulation 259/93 on the monitoring of waste transfers envisages this, but only at a state level.

[44]   The justifications of Article 30 of the Treaty (ex-Article 36) permitting national measures that have restrictive effects on the free movement of goods were extended by European case law to include measures prompted by pressing Community concerns, among which is environmental protection. Cf. CJEC, 20.2.1979, aff. 120/78 Cassis de Dijon, ECR p. 649 and CJEC of 7 February 1985, aff. 240/83, ADBHU, ECR p. 531. This case law was later consolidated, in particular by the Danish bottles case (CJEC 20.9/1988, aff.302/86, ECR p.4607).

[45]   This possibility is spelled out by the two main foundations of the measures concerning waste: when the provisions are based on Article 95 of the Treaty (ex-Article 100a), the state can decide *"to maintain national provisions on grounds of major needs referred to in Article 30* (ex-Article 36) *or relating to the protection of the environment or the working environment"*. Article 176 (ex-Article 130t) specifies that *"the protective measures adopted pursuant to Article 175 (ex-Article 130s) shall not prevent any Member State from maintaining or introducing more stringent protective measures"*. It is also provided for in some directives (e.g.: Article 16 of Directive 75/439 of 16 June 1975 on the elimination of waste oils, as amended by Article 1 of Directive 87/101 of 22 December 1986; Article 8 of Directive 78/319 on toxic and dangerous waste; Article 6§6 of Directive 94/62 of 20 December 1994 on packaging waste).

environmental protection and, on the other, they do not discriminate against the products or producers of another Member State.

The implementation of this exemption shows that there is still friction between the rules protecting the internal market and those protecting the environment, between the economy and the environment[46]. The role of the Community judge is essential in the appraisal of waivers and there appears to be a tendency to check whether a measure is necessary to achieving the aim, rather than its proportionality[47]. In the famous "Walloon waste" case, where the question was to decide on the legitimacy of a regional measure aiming to prohibit the storage of waste from other regions on the region's territory, the European Court of Justice took into account the individual situation of a region and the environmental risks. At the time of the facts, the European Union had not yet legislated on such matters. The Walloon Region, which was responsible for waste management, therefore had every right to draw up its own provisions, provided they complied with the Treaty. But in this case the measure appeared to violate the principle of free movement of goods. To decide whether or not the Walloon measure was non-discriminatory, the European judge took account of the individual circumstances: firstly, waste cannot be treated as any old goods, secondly, and above all, the Court considered the specific situation of the region concerned. In this case, *"the limited capacities"* of the Walloon Region for eliminating waste and the *"massive and abnormal"* character of the influx of waste into the region at the time made the measure taken justifiable[48].

But such tolerance of specific measures to protect the environment is not systematic, even if the European judge stated in a judgement of 22 June 2000 that "Community legislation in the field of the environment does not envisage complete harmonisation"[49].

---

[46] CJCE 23 May 2000, Aff C209/98 Sydhavnens Sten & Grus ApS and Kobenhavns Kommune. See too Aff. C203/96 Chemische Afvalstoffen Dusseldorp BV e.a./Minister van Volkshwisvesting.

[47] "The New Generation Case Law on trade and environment", N. NOTARO, European Law Review, 5 Oct. 2000, p.467-491.

[48] Cf. CJEC on 9 July 1992, aff C2/90 Commission against Belgium, ECR I p. 4431, pts 30 to 36.

[49] CJEC on 22 June 2000, aff. C318/98 Giancarlo Fornasar et al.. In this case, the relevant domestic authorities were allowed to extend the description of "dangerous waste" to include waste not appearing on the list adopted by Council Decision 94/904, in order to apply the stricter protective measures that were necessary in the given context.

2.   To strengthen the integrated approach

Exemptions from common rules are always assessed in the light of the rules of the market, whereas the fact that the principles of integration and sustainable development have a prominent place in the Treaty would suggest instead that the rules of the market should be assessed in the light of social and environmental interests. An integrated approach to waste management in fact leads to encouragement being given to extending the possibilities of exemption from the rules of the market.

In fact, all the measures initiated by regional authorities or which permit the inclusion of environmental concerns in territorial development policies must be encouraged. To help set up the appropriate tools, it may be a good idea, for example, to increase the possibilities of regional aid when they aim to strengthen technical means and the viability of processing and elimination facilities that fulfil the requirements of European law. The Treaty already provides for exemptions from the ban on government aid which distorts or threatens to distort competition (Article 87§1, ex-Article 92). These exemptions are permitted, among other things, to help the development of the less-favoured regions, as well as to ensure environmental protection[50].

But the preventive and integrated approach needs to go further because clashes between the policies followed also must be avoided; on the contrary, a synergy between them must be created, with the aim of sustainable development. Commercial and agricultural policy encourages the excessive packing necessary for transport and product conservation of the products by encouraging agri-food production on a large scale and the sale of products hundreds or thousands of kilometres from their place of production. The disposal of packaging waste near the place of production is obviously excluded in such circumstances. Regional markets should, on the contrary, be supported so as to allow short distribution lines. Similarly, as regards energy policy, it would be advisable to encourage energy saving while at the same time helping local owners of waste elimination facilities to tool up so as to be able to increase the recovery of energy resulting from the incineration of waste or from rubbish tip gases. Incorporating the problems of waste into other policies provides gains on two levels: (i) development and (ii) strengthening environmental protection.

---

[50]   Community framework for state aid for environmental protection (OJ C 37, 3.2.2001 p. 3).

In its search for a balance between unity and respect for diversity and between safeguarding the market and safeguarding the environment, the European Community can no longer favour only one of the interests safeguarded interests, namely a free market unified by common rules. In this context, it has to give way to the regional approach, which appears particularly relevant. More geographical than political, more horizontal than sectoral, favourable to the creation of synergy between the actors on the ground and adapted to a given context, the involvement of the regions opens up a whole field of possibilities for integration on two levels, both environmental and political, provided that the regions themselves become fully aware of their potential in this area.

From the point of view of environmental protection, the regional approach facilitates the integration of waste management into other policies, thereby respecting the principles defended by the European Union, which are a response to the increasing expectations of European citizens (namely sustainable development, improved living standards and the safeguarding of the environment and health). At a political level, the territorial integration of the European Union can only be achieved at the cost of violating the uniform application of European law. The specific structural, political, socio-economic or geographical conditions of each region are realities which must be taken into account. Unless this is done there is a risk of the people concerned enduring integration into the European Union under sufferance and feeling that European integration is something arbitrary that is incompatible with their own identity. In this respect, the negotiations on the accession of the countries of central and eastern Europe probably herald additional distortions. The environmental situation of the states knocking on the EU's door will certainly require exemptions from the common rules. Steps will have to be taken to ensure that adjustments of common rules to take account of a regional context are no longer assessed in the light of the rules of the marketplace but are justified by a "social and environmental conditionality" with an eye on sustainable development.

Jose Miranda Bonilla, University of Seville

Community Regional Policy and its impact on Andalusia

The overall aim of this study is to give an account of regional policy drawn up in Brussels and assess the impact of this policy on a region in great need of funding - Andalusia. More specifically, the study sets out to do the following:

1. Study the theoretical approaches which underlie Community regional policy and look at how these are applied in practice when it comes to creating specific aid instruments and deciding on the distribution of the Structural Funds between the different countries.

2. Determine to what extent the State's regional policy is dependent on the Community, in terms of both theoretical approaches and financial resources.

3. Assess the importance attached by central government to the problem of regional disparities in Spain, comparing investment in, and aid received by, the different Autonomous Communities.

4. Analyse the economic planning of regional government and how this is influenced by the requirements of Community regional policy.

5. Quantify the relative weight of Structural Fund income in the Andalusian economy.

6. Analyse sectoral distribution of investment financed with Community aid.

7. Evaluate the territorial impact of this investment.

The working hypothesis assumed that Community regional policy would constitute the main element of Spanish regional policy. Central government would be limited to channelling Community funds, sparing itself a large part of the budgetary effort required to fulfil the constitutional mandate of reducing regional disparities. It was

67

also assumed that funding was totally insufficient, both at Community and State level, and that in terms of territorial distribution, the correlation between income level and amount of aid was not as just as one might hope, to a large extent because of the Community tradition of sharing out scarce funds between all parties, a tradition also followed by Spain at national level.

In the case of Andalusia, the study set out with the assumption that an excessively high percentage of Community aid was exclusively channelled into the funding of infrastructure, and very little directly into production. Furthermore, it was sensed that there was a policy of concentrating actions in favour of those centres in Andalusia which were the strongest, contrary to one of the objectives that has constantly been brandished by the Autonomous Community government - reducing disparities within regions.

The study is divided into two parts. The first part aims to given an overview of and explain Community regional policy. The second part focuses on how this policy is applied in Andalusia. In total, there are eight chapters, in addition to this introduction.

The first chapter aims to give a brief overview of the European Community. We thought it would be a good idea to sum up how the EC started and developed, making it easier to understand the way in which one of its policies - regional policy - is formulated. It can therefore be seen as an introductory chapter.

In the second chapter we look at the history of regional policy. We thought we should explain how Community regional policy has developed, following the distinct phases that are apparent in its short history. This chapter contains many of the keys that will improve out understanding of how regional policy functions.

The third chapter focuses on the analysis of the regional issue in Europe. Subjects covered include the formation of the regional map and its characteristics; the situation of the regions with respect to the main socio-economic indicators; and, lastly, the trends that are emerging as the regions develop. The aim was to pinpoint those factors which justify the formulation of a regional policy at Community level. Particular reference is made at all times to Andalusia, to improve understanding of its position in the European regional context.

The last chapter of the first part explains about the different instruments which can be used to shape regional policy, including other sector-based Community policies, with the aim of defining the different elements that go to make up a fairly complex system of rules.

After looking at the Community situation and its regional policy we enter fully into the second part, which focuses on the situation in Andalusia.

In chapter five we analyse what has formed the basis of economic policy in Andalusia - regional planning. An analysis is given of the different plans which have shaped the guidelines for development in Andalusia in recent years, assessing the different objectives, strategies, results, political attitudes, etc. We compare some plans with others, as well as with other development programmes of other European regions. This chapter helps us understand the bases of the actions financed with Community funds in our region.

Chapter six studies the different programmes and main projects funded by the ERDF in the period in question. All programmes that have actually started are covered, but are not all dealt with in the same way, since they are not all of equal importance. Those which are less relevant are assessed more superficially, while others are analysed in more detail. The programmes we focus on have a higher level of investment, are better designed, or in some cases are of interest because of their type of management. The vast number of projects carried out made it impossible to perform a detailed study of each and every one. In most cases they were studied together, and a sectoral assessment made; this was especially the case for road projects, which accounted for most of the projects studied.

Chapter seven covers the overall assessment of all completed projects and programmes. A financial assessment was carried out first, to determine the extent of ERDF funding in Andalusia in the period concerned, in relation to other public funding and the regional economic dynamics. We also assessed the sectoral impact of these projects and programmes, to determine which sectors have been strengthened and which ones marginalised by these support mechanisms. Finally, the territorial impact of Community regional policy on our region is assessed.

The last chapter contains our final conclusions and proposals for improving the management and efficiency of implementation of Community regional policy in future years.

The main conclusions reached are as follows:

The first point to stress is that Community regional policy has become a key instrument for tackling development in Andalusia. Its effect on our region goes beyond the mere transfer of funds. The thinking behind European policy has become the benchmark for regional policy throughout Andalusia. Generally speaking, this has had a positive effect; however, we should not forget the change of direction this brought about in the policies followed by the Autonomous Community, and the extremely uncritical attitude with which we adopted many of these ideas.

Community regional policy has served to consolidate planning as an instrument for regional development, just when the most militant neoliberalism rejected any state intervention in the orientation of development. These years of EC membership and, above all, the implementation of Structural Fund reform, have resulted in a fairly good programming culture. We must immediately add, however, that the necessary flexibility of the programming documents has in some cases served as an alibi for cancelling or definitively shelving a great many plans and programmes, thereby invalidating the whole process.

We also have Community regional policy to thank for keeping the regional question alive at European and state level. Without this Community reference, ideas on the correction of regional disparities in Spain would probably have been abandoned or, at the very least, not taken seriously. The unresolved - and probably unresolvable - issue of autonomous financing could mask the issue of Spanish regional policy.

As for the funding we have received, it has to be said that this has been substantial - much more than we could have imagined in the early years. This funding has provided a vital financial boost to the investment required to modernise the Andalusian economy. The effects of the almost 400,000 million pesetas received over eight years were certainly felt in a region like Andalusia. However, it must be pointed out that this high volume of funding obscures the fact that our region, despite coming bottom in all European rankings, actually received much lower levels of funding than other regions and countries. One might say that we have not been treated correctly or fairly, since the ERDF subsidies per inhabitant are much lower than most of the Objective 1 regions.

This low level of funding has meant that the impact of the ERDF has been felt less at macro-economic level in Andalusia. We have seen that its impact has been less than half of that in Greece, Ireland or Portugal.

As for distribution by sector, we have seen how infrastructure absorbed a percentage of funding higher than the European average. This enabled our transport infrastructure to be renovated in an amazingly short space of time. The modernisation of the major transport routes in just a few years rapidly changed the image of Andalusia from that of an almost third-world region to that of a true European space. This tangible reality also had its downside, but that does not mean it should be rejected. The first point to note is that the improvement of the major routes was carried out in many cases at the expense of the secondary network. Also, the quality of much of the work has suffered considerably, and just a few years after it was first put into use a number of striking defects have become apparent. Some of the new funding will therefore have to be allocated to the maintenance and repair of these projects. In some cases investment was made without reviewing the spatial planning which must go hand-in-hand with any new infrastructure. Thus, we see motorways superimposed on road networks that were previously criticised and that are now being unquestioningly reinforced.

It should not be forgotten that funding allocated to improving infrastructure was necessarily money not spent on other sectors. In the case of Andalusia, transport was rapidly improved at the expense of direct subsidies to the productive sector, for which reason we have neglected our businesses more than those who preferred to improve infrastructure more slowly, providing more support to the productive fabric.

The lack of attention paid to the productive system and lack of dedicated funds has meant that Andalusia has made little progress in the process of convergence with Spanish and European levels. The region has not managed to improve its position in terms of income per head with regard to the national average, and continues to stand at around half the European average, despite the slight progress made in the last few years. In the case of Ireland, for example, the level of income has gone up 10 points in relation to the Community average. Andalusia, on the other hand has alternated

71

between periods of improvement and slight decline. And if there has been no convergence in terms of income, in terms of unemployment it is even more flagrant. The main problem afflicting our Autonomous Community continues to be unemployment, which we seem to be unable to resolve or find any solutions to whatsoever.

As regards the territorial impact there has been some success, as we have already seen, in the application of territorial strategies within Andalusia. However, we have also shown what happens if there is no clear territorial model. The actions of central and regional governments are not based on the same territorial thinking but on quite opposite approaches. Moreover, we also show how there have been many regions in which Community aid has hardly been felt at all.

Lastly, we draw attention to management problems. Most Community resources continue to be managed from Madrid, despite the fact that there is no apportionment of powers to account for this superiority over the Autonomous Community administration. Centralist mechanisms continue to oppose greater - let alone full - participation of the autonomous regions in the management of Community aid. The current division of competences between the two administrative levels has not guaranteed the levels of coordination required to apply Community regional policy in our territory in a more coherent and effective manner.

Based on our findings, and on the experience acquired throughout the course of the study, we have ventured to formulate a series of proposals aimed at improving the effectiveness of EU regional policy actions in our Community. This is how we intend to bring our work of analysis, diagnostic and proposals to an end.

We shall start with economic planning. Let us reiterate that we must pledge our commitment to planning as the best way of managing regional development in Andalusia. We must start to talk of plans which work from the bottom up, following the "down-top" approach which has been successfully applied in other countries. What we suggest is to open up planning processes where the concerns of all partners involved are noted before any specific proposals are drawn up, and used as a basis for discussing a concerted strategy, resulting in a number of clear objectives and projects which put them into practice.

Moving on to the sectoral distribution of expenditure, we must start by drawing attention to the need to reduce investment in infrastructure. As we have already seen, Spain - and particularly Andalusia - has invested most of its resources in roads, following the Italian policy for the Mezzogiorno region, which has had so little impact. It is now time to plead for a better balance between the creation of infrastructure and support for the productive system.

One fundamental aspect is the management of aid. In view of the failures and errors observed, we attempt to suggest a series of measures to improve management, bring EU action closer to citizens and increase efficiency. We would first stress the need for better coordination of all the Structural Funds and all other Community financial instruments. A second question would be that of keeping isolated projects to a minimum; an effort must be made to integrate all actions into programmes. "Integrate" is meant here in the strict sense of the term: we are not talking about mere groupings of unrelated projects. The other formula to promote is that of global subsidies, which have proved to be the best mechanisms for channelling Community aid to the productive machinery. In addition to the IFA, other intermediary organisations could manage these subsidies for a more specific area or for a given type of sectoral action.

We would also stress the need to find a new balance between the part of the MAC which comes under the responsibility of the central government and that of regional government. In our opinion, where there is a wide range of powers, it does not make sense for central government to keep more than 20% of ERDF funding - a percentage which will basically be used for national road infrastructure projects and other specific actions coming under, once again, the responsibility of central government. One can fall into the trap of duplicating administrations, which do not act to promote the most rapid and effective regional development, and frequently show a lack of interest in coordination and boosting synergy. In addition, in many cases, central administration control does not comply with the additionality criteria imposed by Brussels, for it is not uncommon for the same programmes that are implemented in regions receiving both state and ERDF funding to be carried out in other areas under exactly the same financial conditions, even though the State is obliged to double its contribution if ERDF funding cannot be granted. Therefore, the regional level should be able to reckon with at least 80% of the funding. It would also be a good idea to incorporate all actions of local councils into the sphere of regional administration. Coordination between actions at regional and local level would thus be easier and more productive than has been the case until now.

However, the necessary process of decentralisation would not end with the transfer of resources from state to regional level. Intermediate regional bodies need to be set up, which would manage the regional share of funding, creating local or regional infrastructure and, above all, channelling aid into the regional productive fabric. We could follow the example of the "CEDER" centres set up under the Leader initiative. Although the activity of the CEDERs focused on sharing out the global subsidy to support the maintenance and creation of companies, the idea is to broaden their powers. In the same way that they may know the most about the economic and business situation on the ground in their region, they are also the best placed to know what is most lacking in terms of minor road, water, environmental, infrastructure etc. With the allocation of a proportion of funding to each region, in accordance with its population and surface area, but also taking into account criteria related to territorial balance, we would succeed in bringing the administration of Community funding closer to the population, and also guarantee that the whole of Andalusia would receive a share of European aid. This is essential if we are to get the development project for Andalusia off the ground and extend it throughout the region. The operation of these centres will need to be monitored, and part of the funding put aside in order to reward those which prove to be the most dynamic and capable of generating the most investment. With time, these structures could serve as a basis for consolidating the idea of a sound regional structure which would acquire its own political and administrative powers.

Another very important question is that of changing the criteria according to which funding is allocated to the different regions. It is clear that Andalusia receives less than it would if simply objective distribution criteria- not even criteria designed to ensure balance - were applied. As we have seen, the region's large size and limited decision-making powers has considerably reduced its funding possibilities. For the coming years, we should change to a system of allocation of resources agreed by consensus, whereby scales with minimum and maximum percentages for the allocation of resources from the Funds are established. The link between the Structural Funds and the issue of autonomous financing should be abolished, while continuing to uphold the principle of additionality. Allocation criteria could be the same as those used in the allocation of the Inter-Regional Compensation Fund according to the most recent regulations, although they could be improved by increasing the importance of the unemployment criterion. More importance could also be given to income levels. This would lead to a fairer distribution of resources, in which Andalusia would receive almost 40% of the Structural Funds granted to Spain under Objective 1. Similarly, we should strive to ensure that there is a greater concentration of Structural Funds for the Objective 1 regions than for Objectives 2 and 5b, as it is in Objective 1 regions that the Spanish regional problems really lie. Objective 2 and 5b regions in many cases serve merely as pretexts for making sure that Community funding is channelled into all regions, something very commendable on the part of the Spanish government, provided that this does not result in funding being diverted from the poorest regions to the richest. However, what is most serious is that defining type 2 or 5b regions in our country means that we cannot then argue in Brussels as vociferously as we should for the principle of concentration to be reinforced. This will be particularly serious with the arrival of the new countries into the EU, all of which will probably be classed under Objective 1, with the larger Member States refusing to increase the budget for structural policies. We should therefore champion the cause of those in favour of regional policy being aimed at the regions with real problems. This approach will in the long term benefit Spain as a whole more than the one adopted so far, which is characterised by a very limited view of things and is clearly influenced by those regions which have a vested interest in this approach, as well as more political influence than other regions.

To bring all this about, we are aware that the attitude of regional government must change. Andalusia's demographic weight has not been matched by its political weight. Moreover, the exponential increase of the Structural Funds in recent years and the fact that we are one of its main recipients owing to our region's large size, constitute the ideal pretext for using this issue as an element of political propaganda. Basically the underlying idea has been that we have been very well treated, that the Structural Funds constitute a "cushy number" and that it is better not to draw attention to the issue at all, lest it should occur to somebody to thoroughly review the system. For that reason, we should all make a point of finding out what we are entitled to, and claim our rights with greater conviction.

Finally, as part of this chapter of proposals, we must defend the need for evaluation as the best method of ensuring the proper management and impact of Community aid. We must impose the culture of assessing public actions. We must improve our knowledge of the effects of the different projects on regional development, in order to identify those which are of the most interest and those which should be shelved. We must rationalise the management of resources and justify all actions that are funded with public money. For that, the first thing to do is to facilitate the transparency of this management.

With the information available, it will be easier to assess ex-ante, on-going and ex-post programmes. The three are equally necessary. We should move towards independent, impartial assessment of government if this is genuinely not to serve as a means of "buying" consent for a political action. Probably the best way would be for the Commission to appoint teams of external assessors, if possibly from different States, thus ensuring maximum impartiality.

When we see that assessment serves to improve public action, we will be on the right track towards serious management of regional development.

1999/2000

EUROPE OF THE NEXT CENTURY: HOW CAN REGIONS AND CITIES CONTRIBUTE TO ENHANCING DEMOCRACY IN THE EU?

Chairman of the jury

Ms Mercedes Bresso (IT), President of the Province of Turin

Theses submitted

NUMBER OF ENTRANTS	LANGUAGES		COUNTRY	
23	7	German English Spanish Finnish French Italian Swedish	9	Germany Austria Spain Finland France Ireland Italy United Kingdom Sweden

Winners

First prize:

Dr Alessia Damonte (IT), *The regions, the state and the European Union: is a "third level" emerging? - Italian negotiations on cohesion policies for 2000-2006: the case of Objective 2 regions*, University of Milan

Second prize:

Dr Elisa Roller (NL), *Catalonia and European integration: A regionalist strategy for nationalist objectives*, Department of Government, London School of Economics

compensate for the loss of Objective 1 resources also reinforced the expectation during national negotiations that the general redistributive criteria that had been established during the adoption procedure could be materially altered by applying political pressure when the programming documents were presented. In other words, if a strong case were made for specific local economic situations, the Commission would naturally grant the relative dispensations.

Nonetheless, following a number of major innovations in recent years, representatives from the Italian institutions have been able to adapt their organisational machinery, and this has had an impact on both the implementation phase (e.g. by improving structural fund spending capacity) and the preparatory phase (e.g. by improving coordination between the various tiers of government during the policy formulation phase for the 2000-2006 period).

The guiding thread of this change seems to have been, and still be, the need (as promoted by an "integrationist" elite within central government) to bring national structures and policy into line with European-level demands in response to increasingly binding supranational ties.

During the previous negotiation period, Italy's objective was to meet the macro-economic parameters established at Maastricht and national resources were therefore transferred from development policies to economic policies. Greater importance was therefore given to European aid for micro-economic intervention. Now that the special assistance for the Mezzogiorno has come to an end, there have been moves at national level to rationalise development policies according to the new concept of "deprived area". This is essentially in line with the "'European" definition of areas eligible for public assistance, i.e. "objective" areas, drawn up by DG Regional Policy, and "state aid" areas, which come under DG Competition. While this "rationalised" intervention officially reaffirmed the Europeanisation of development policies, it also presented an opportunity - and revealed the need - to change the way in which decision-making powers were allocated, since it implicitly recognised that the possession of technical information was a new and specific legitimate resource.

Recognition of this new resource could help to redefine the institutional approach to this policy area as it opens it up to players whose competitive approach differs from that of the "inter-governmental" elite which guided previous negotiations. However, if the potential resource of "technical knowledge" is to become a reality, a committed "entrepreneurial" subject is required. This seems to be the role of the new Department for Development Policies and Cohesion (DPS) which is part of the new Ministry of the Treasury, Budget and Economic Programming. The DPS is the organisational response of the "integrationist" elite (who promote European-style "structural adjustment" of the institutions) to the need for initiatives and technical coordination for planning. This coordination is needed not only upwards towards centralised European decision-making, or horizontally vis-à-vis the sphere of competence of the various departments of central government, but also downwards towards local and regional authorities. In terms of subsidiarity, Article 5 of the 1997 Constitution officially recognises local and regional authorities as co-decision-makers in this policy area. Now that such bodies are finally being included, structural policy, even in Italy, is increasingly becoming one of the areas that best embodies Monnet's implicit project to create a form of European *governance* which mobilises, and gives joint responsibility to, stakeholders at local level, bringing them together in broad, mutually dependent decision-making networks that cooperate to promote development synergies.

The new national decision-making body's strategy vis-à-vis both sub-national bodies and the Commission thus focuses on technical support and proposals. Where sub-national bodies are concerned, it acts as a regulatory agency that draws up general rules. Where the Commission is concerned, however, it acts as a direct and "functional" partner outside the diplomatic channel. In short, the aim is to create a genuine "administrative channel" that brings together "federal", national and sub-national levels through problem-solving activities, designing and implementing solutions that are the most effective economically and the least dependent on short-term political considerations.

The effectiveness of development aid also depends on information about local policy issues. Only the "lower" tiers of government possess this information; if the higher tiers managed such information, it would result in lower quality and an information overload. Because of this, the "top-priority" institutional structure promoted by this "integrationist" elite ideally hinges on vertical interaction according to "hierarchical co-ordination". However, this hierarchy should no longer be legitimised (solely) by its monopoly on the "production of law"; but also (and above all) by its possession of the skills and information necessary for resolving collective issues. However, attempts to make interactions more innovative in a very short space of time collided with the expectations that these consolidated procedures had created. During programme negotiations, the Commission, whose position had been strengthened by more centralised decision-making, effectively refused to recognise the legitimacy of Italy's proposal to manage Structural Funds according to "socio-economic" units (i.e. local labour systems) rather than administrative units, since they were a more effective response to changing local realities and development issues. This proposal was basically rejected because it was only presented to the Commission via the technical channels and not via diplomatic and "official" channels. DG XVI therefore viewed this as part of the recurring Italian trend to try and skirt around European regulations.

Different regions, however, reacted differently to the obligations of this new phase of coordination.

2. Objective 2: Regions of north-central Italy

The decision-making process promoted by the "integrationist" elite was based on the principle of "selective assistance"; it therefore gave the regional authorities responsibility for setting regional interests and thereby implicitly made them the legitimate representatives of these interests and the decision-makers fully responsible for managing the region. In order for relations to be fully restructured, however, these authorities somehow needed to become proponents of economic rather than political efficiency. This is what the national body sought to achieve by co-opting regional experts and familiarising them with their way of thinking.

This process met with fierce opposition from Objective 2 regions, even early on in the new regulation adoption process, as for the first time these regions were committed to solving problems via a consensual and autonomous process using their own technical task-force. The regions of north-central Italy considered these mechanisms to be not only economically punishing but also detrimental to the autonomy that the "inter-governmental" elite had granted them during previous negotiations (i.e. distributive mechanisms that favoured a "pork-barrel" approach to EU funding and were managed by a Commission that was still seeking legitimacy). In response to this, they used the two contrasting forms of legitimisation provided by the "inter-governmental" and "integrationist" elite to arrogate their right to decide autonomously how resources should be distributed between and inside regions. This refusal to accept the type of coordination proposed by the national body resulted in genuine horizontal negotiations. These were headed by the Objective 2 regions who once again recognised the "inter-governmental" elite as important players at national level and reverted to the pork-barrel approach and informal contacts with the Commission in an attempt to justify their choices rather than those of the "integrationist" elite. As a result, resources were redistributed according to Pareto's principles of efficiency and so as to maintain a consensus. This had the additional advantage of dividing up beneficiary areas by following pro forma the integrationist elite's proposal to base calculations on local labour systems rather than provinces. However, the Commission continued to base its proposals on the latter - i.e. official NUTS III level regions - which would have led to the Objective 2 programme being ruled ineligible. When DG XVI did indeed rule this programme ineligible, the centralised decision-making promoted by the integrationist elite, which had been denied by the Objective 2 regions, was restored - albeit inadvertently.

3.   **Objective 1: the Mezzogiorno**

Where Objective 1 regions were concerned, however, the "integrationist" elite's project was partially achieved as these regions were included in vertical negotiating tables. Here programming was drawn up more or less by consensus and European ties were strengthened during supranational negotiations.

The Catania Seminar in December 1998 - which some national officials defined as a milestone and which was, without doubt, extremely innovative - marked the start of consultations, which were later reaffirmed in preparatory documents for the Community Support Framework. In fact, it was in Catania that the lengthy document "One hundred ideas for development" was presented, containing proposals drawn up by Ministries, regional authorities, interest groups' associations and a network of experts who made comments and suggestions based on their research. The seminar was therefore the first occasion when potential development guidelines for Italy and, in particular, the Mezzogiorno were actually discussed.

After Catania the work continued at various levels across Italy. At central government level, a number of sector-specific negotiating tables were set up with a view to drafting documents and proposals which were successively translated into actions at national level for the 2000-2006 period. At regional level, sector-specific negotiating tables resulted in interim programme reports containing proposals by regional social partners, even if some of these proposals were still in their early stages. The fact that the regions met the programme deadlines and - more importantly - that there was real commitment to regional-level programming shows to what extent it was possible to mobilise within the regions themselves resources and knowledge which until then had been overlooked.

As a result of negotiations between the different tiers of government (i.e. state, regions and European Union) during 1999 and 2000, the Community Support Framework was approved in August 2000. For the first time, Italian Objective 1 areas were among the first to be given the go-ahead by the European Union.

3.1   Consultations in the Italian regions of Campania, Calabria and Puglia

But what did the involvement of regional partners mean for the various areas of the Mezzogiorno? A number of pointers can be drawn from the cases of Campania, Calabria and Puglia, starting with the similarities between these regions.

Firstly, in recent years all three regions have increased their knowledge of Community programmes. Indeed, one of the first consequences of the consultations was that they reinforced the regional dimension of many professional associations. For example, it is due to the 2000-2006 programme alone that in Calabria the Confindustria (Confederation of Italian Industry) acquired proper regional offices and the technical knowledge necessary for drawing up local development guidelines and/or suggestions. Until recently, regional offices were merely symbolic and were not involved in strategic planning concerning the organisation's role in economic development at regional level. In Puglia, whose economy is more prosperous and, more importantly, less dependent on the public sector, the local Confindustria has been more attentive to regional and, therefore, company demands. In 1994, in cooperation with a number of banks, it set up a bank and company monitoring centre, the role of which is to monitor companies' training needs and help match (at least from an analytical point of view) employment demand and supply.

Secondly, the need to provide instruments for gauging (and thus promoting) socio-economic development in the region prompted governing bodies to join forces and set up an integrated regional "system" aimed at enhancing existing skills in the region. In almost all the aforementioned regions, the first drafts of the Regional Operational Plans (the so-called Interim Reports) were written in cooperation with representatives of universities, research bodies and interest groups. In-depth discussions were subsequently held concerning public policy adoption methods, something which until then had been rare, if not altogether non existent

The programming for the 2000-2006 period therefore helped to set up a genuine regional planning "system" that brought together representatives of trade unions, business, the crafts sector, and agriculture with a view to adopting development programmes that will determine regional socio-economic life for the next ten years.

Finally, another key factor - which is completely innovative and therefore harder to assess - is the inclusion of interest groups that had previously been ignored, such as "non-profit" organisations and consumer associations. Representatives of voluntary organisations (who are brought together at national and regional level under the Third Sector Forum) were involved throughout the drafting of the regional operational plans and - according to a number of key people we interviewed - with a considerable degree of mutual satisfaction. Community programming mechanisms have thus helped extend the circle of local interest groups, even in areas where civil society had not had a high profile in the past. There are, of course, a number of significant differences between these three regions. Firstly, the degree to which interest groups are equipped to mediate varies according to the level of economic development in each region. As has already been pointed out, Puglia has a higher regional GDP and lower level of unemployment than the other regions under discussion and is better equipped to meet Community requirements. Not only is the local economic system capable of making the most of Community funding opportunities (albeit in a manner that is at times open to question) but also, and more importantly, local economic players (i.e. businessmen, trade unionists, craftsmen and farmers' representatives) demonstrate a dynamism often lacking in other areas of southern Italy. It is no coincidence that the bank and company monitoring centre was set up in Puglia and only later extended to Basilicata and, more recently still, Calabria.

Secondly, administrative capacities also vary considerably. A recent POLEIS survey revealed where there were delays in programming and implementing specific measures aimed at extending the decision-making and management role of the regional authorities. Even in November 2000, almost four years after the law

Elisa Roller, London School of Economics

Catalonia and European Integration:
a regionalist strategy for nationalist objectives?

Introduction

Since Spanish accession to the European Community in 1986, the nationalist-led Catalan government, the *Generalitat*, has successfully managed to secure a growing role for itself in the process of European integration. This has been achieved by a multiple strategy incorporating an intense process of nation-building together with a pragmatic political approach aimed at reforming policy making mechanisms at both the Spanish and European levels.

To analyze this strategy, the thesis provides several levels of explanation. First, it focuses on the pro-European element of Catalan nationalist discourse and how this has been transferred to a series of policy objectives. This pro-European vision is a present-day terminological and ideological substitute for the traditional objectives of modernising and transforming the Spanish state, inherent in Catalan nationalist discourse. These objectives also include the pursuit of the legal/constitutional recognition of the plurinational and multilinguistic composition of both the Spanish state and the European Union (EU). Second, the consolidation of this pro-Europeanism within the Catalan nationalist ideology is explored through the activities of Catalonia's nationalist led government - the Generalitat - and specifically that of *Convergència i Unió (CiU)*, the centre-right nationalist party which has dominated Catalan politics for nearly two decades. Despite this pro-Europeanism, the thesis concludes that for a variety of reasons, many Catalan nationalists have increasingly become disillusioned with the so-called "Europe of the Regions" for a variety of reasons.

Third, the process by which the pro-European dimension has been exercised at institutional and policy levels is also traced with an overview of Catalan participation in the EU policy-making process. This includes the establishment of a network of EU affairs offices both in Brussels and throughout Catalonia, the prominence of Catalan leaders in various EU and extra-EU institutions, and the steady increase in Catalan participation in the formulation, implementation and monitoring of EU regional policy.

Finally and more generally, the purpose of this thesis is to explore the changing role of sub-national authorities within the process of European integration and the adaptation of nationalist movements to the challenges posed by this process by presenting the case study of Catalonia. The thesis highlights the importance of nationalist movements in the growing role of the regions or sub-national levels of government and their pursuance individual policy priorities, by attempting to circumvent national state governments. The effects these efforts have had, as the Catalan case illustrates, reflect a fundamental change in the domestic policy-making process. This change has occurred in part as a result of sub-national pressures but also as a result of the Europeanisation of the policy-making process.

Background

The traditional concept of the nation-state within the European Union is being challenged at present it is alleged, by two forces, one emerging from the process of European integration and the other force in the form of regionalist/nationalist movements strengthening their presence on the domestic and international scene. As a result, more emphasis has been placed on the role of the regions within the EU, in part because of the administrative and political decentralised arrangements in federal and quasi-federal member states such as Belgium, Germany, Austria and Spain. In light of increased co-operation between the EU and the sub-national authorities, will this association result in the undoing of the structure and function of the nation-state as it has been traditionally viewed? How will regions with high degrees of autonomy and self-government within their own states be able to influence the EU decision-making process faced by resistance to the devolution or transfer of policy-making powers to any institution which does not directly represent the state? How will moderate nationalist ideology reconcile its own nation-forming objectives with a shift towards adopting federalist institutional arrangements and practices in a supranational political system? Are these two objectives compatible or will they inevitably conflict? And in legal and constitutional terms, why is it that the implementation of EU legislation on member-states has a relatively clear set of procedures and the same process is so lacking for sub-national authorities?

These questions have a special significance for Spain as the process of European integration coincides with the creation and evolution over the last two decades of the State of Autonomies, a radically different model from the one that has prevailed in Spain since the eighteenth century Spain, more so than any other member-state of the EU, has been experiencing a change both in its internal political structure and in its exterior political outlook, ending nearly four decades of political and cultural marginalisation from the rest of Europe. Although the strength and nature of regionalism vary within the member-states of the EU, an analysis of the Catalan case within Spain and the EU framework provides a strong example of the changing role of the regions and other sub-national authorities within the emerging European political system. This role will likely increase in the future, as sub-national units have grown faster than the state at the central level (Sharpe, 1988).

Examining the parallel relationships between the Catalan and Spanish governments on the one hand and the Catalan government and the EU on the other hand explains the ongoing development of a process of institutional and political legitimisation for the European Union and Catalonia. This process is fundamentally transforming traditional interpretations of the nation-state. By engaging in competitive relationships based on the pursuit of political and economic benefits within the state, both Catalonia and the EU hope to be able to continue with the analogous processes of state building (in the case of the EU) and nation formation (in the case of Catalonia). Thus, the Catalan case questions pre-conceived notions about the role of sub-national authorities in the process of European integration. Furthermore, as the process of European integration deepens and increasingly affects citizens' day to day lives, the Catalan case could prove to be a model followed by other European regions or sub-national authorities. Its high degree of self-government and its unique strategy in dealing with EU matters has set a precedent for nationalist movements attempting to cope with the Europeanisation of politics and policy-making.

The Catalan case also demonstrates how the progress made towards European integration has changed the nature of Catalan nationalism. Wilson and Smith (1993) have argued that this progress towards integration has led to the birth of new ideas and concepts about regional culture, ethnic identities, and nationhood. Besides 'Europeanising' the Catalan nationalist movement, the process of European integration has also been a key motivating factor in moves towards institutional change. The relationship between key actors has changed and there has been a recomposition of governance in the Spanish political system. As new processes evolve, these have thrown traditional methods of policy formulation and implementation into disarray. These processes include decentralisation (central government to regional government), centralisation (central government to the European Commission), principles of subsidiarity (European Commission to regional government), and supra-national institutional building. The issue of Europeanisation will be dealt with in the next section.

The Europeanisation of sub-national politics

The twin processes of devolution and Europeanisation have led to the increased importance of "Europe" for the Catalan nationalist movement and particularly, its mainstream political party, *Convergència i Unió* (CiU). In the 1990s, disappointment in the performance of the Committee of the Regions may have temporarily diverted attention elsewhere as did the negotiations between CiU and the ruling Spanish conservative party, the *Partido Popular* (PP) following the 1996 general election. Nevertheless, the advent of Spain's participation in the single currency, worries about enlargement and continued exposure to the process of European integration have led CiU to refocus its energies towards building Catalonia's profile within the EU and securing its position within the Spanish political system. It has continued to make progress and has attempted to discover innovative methods of securing a greater role for sub-national authorities within the EU's institutional framework. CiU's leverage within the Spanish political system has also allowed it to perform an agenda-setting role in developing Spain's position on European matters. The extent to which this has occurred is difficult to measure in quantitative terms but clearly, Catalonia's contribution has been beyond that of many of the other autonomous communities in Spain.

Nevertheless, there are potential obstacles that could hinder the success achieved by CiU in securing greater participatory rights for itself and other autonomous communities in the EU decision-making process. These might include:

1.   the emergence of an anti-European movement within Catalan society concerned with Catalonia's loss of influence in the process of European integration and the ongoing crises within the EU itself (e.g. the resignation of all 20 EU Commissioners in early 1999);

2.   the potential failure of EMU;

3.   a substantial electoral change eliminating CiU's possibility of wielding power at the domestic political level;

4.   the breakup of CiU's coalition;

5.   the replacement of CiU's political leadership with actors unwilling to commit fully to the present EU strategy;

6.   increased Europeanisation which has not been met by a parallel process of devolution or regionalisation in Spain;

7.   a return to fundamentalist nationalist objectives, rejecting the moderate nature of the Catalan nationalist movement and embracing a more aggressive and less co-operative strategy.

Despite these potential pitfalls, much progress has been made since Spain's entry into the European Community in 1986. First, attitudes towards the participation of sub-national authorities in the process of European integration have changed and nowhere is this more clear than in Spain. Through the years, direct contact with the rest of the EU has not only strengthened the Catalan nationalist movement itself but also changed Spanish political culture. This changing political culture has favoured modifying the existing system of limited participatory measures for sub-national authorities in the EU's policy-making process.

Second, involvement in the process of European integration has allowed Catalonia to incorporate the concept of subsidiarity into its discourse both at home and abroad. Concepts such as subsidiarity in EU parlance have been subject to wide interpretation among sub-national authorities. On the one hand, the concept benefits regions immensely, by theoretically allowing regional governments to claim more power. The development of the principle of subsidiarity meant that the welfare of the regions was no longer an issue to be dealt with exclusively by the member-states themselves. Basque and Catalan nationalist parties such as the Partido Nacionalista Vasco (PNV) and CiU believe that they can reshape the structure and attitudes of the EU so as to benefit them individually as regions. These parties have used the principle of subsidiarity as a defence for the greater distribution of powers at both the European and national levels. The Catalan government has sought to increase existing levels of self-government and to deepen the process of the devolution of competencies not only within the framework of the Spanish state, but also within an association of various member-states that is the EU.

Third, the Catalan government and specifically CiU, with much of its economic ideology based on free-trade and single market principles, have adopted the position that as greater European economic integration evolves, economic interdependence between Catalonia and the rest of Spain will increase (Díez Medrano, 1995). For Catalonia, the EU has offered the benefits of a large single market and generous regional subsidies. In addition, by reinforcing democratic practices and the rules of the free market doctrine, EU membership has helped secure economic reform not only at the regional level, but also within other regions of Spain. EU membership has forced Spain to adopt an enormous amount of competition rules and market regulations, compelling it to embark in much-needed structural reform, the results of which have clearly benefited Catalonia. Furthermore, joining the EU has compelled Spain to pass the political tests of democracy and respect the minority cultures within its borders.

Fourth, the recognition of the high degree of economic interdependence between Catalonia, Spain and the rest of the EU has led the Catalan nationalist movement to pursue a political strategy both at home and abroad based on political interdependence. To a great extent, this has already been achieved through full participation in the Spanish political process. Greater interdependence is seen as a political advantage because it would allow Catalan nationalists to gain greater political control over economic development. In a sense, the rationale behind this strategy is similar to that behind the European integration movement itself: first, set out to achieve control over the economic sphere, then proceed with political integration. As a result, the Catalan nationalist movement has embraced European integration by supporting political integration into the European Union and seeking political autonomy within their own states at the same time.

Fifth, the Catalan nationalist movement's pro-European strategy has allowed it to use the EU as a forum to define its national and international identities. This has contributed to the further transformation of the concept of the nation-state among researchers as well as a functional reinterpretation of the concept of sovereignty. The shift towards European integration "not only threatens the state's sovereignty, it strengthens the EC's role as arbiter of international and inter-regional integration, further calling into question the degree to which joining the EC has transformed or reduced national and/or governmental sovereignty"[1]. In essence, the EU has proved to be a support system for regions seeking greater autonomy. The Commission's support for increased contact with sub-national authorities in areas such as regional policy merely reinforces the legitimacy of regionalism. By doing so and in its efforts to find its own identity, the process of European integration has challenged state sovereignty.

Yet, as the State of Autonomies consolidates and the process of European integration intensifies it is not clear if the mainstream Catalan nationalist movement will remain as cohesive as it has been over the last 20 years. The growing divergence of opinions expressed by Catalan government and party officials on an appropriate EU strategy for Catalonia clearly reflects significant discrepancies on the importance attached to Catalan participation in the process of European integration. Ironically, the fact that European integration presupposes the increasing transfer of competencies from both the sub-national and national to the supra-national level seemingly does not give rise to concern within Catalan political circles.

Nevertheless, Catalonia has been able to compensate for the loss of sovereignty derived from the supranationalisation of competencies, at least in some measure. This has been achieved through the establishment of informal and formal participatory measures in the process of European integration. It is clear that as the process of European integration intensifies and more competencies are transferred to the EU level, Catalonia and other Spanish autonomous communities will in some way want to be compensated. This compensation will have to come in the form of greater participation in EU matters. The justification for this compensation can be made in terms of nationalist rhetoric. However, a more logical explanation can be derived from the issue of administrative and bureaucratic efficiency. If the process of European integration is to maintain a certain standard of efficiency, this will depend to a great extent to the measures used to incorporate the interests and experiences of those responsible for policy implementation, as is the case of sub-national authorities.

---

[1] Wilson, T. and Smith, M. (1993). Cultural Change and the New Europe, Boulder: Westview Press, Inc., pp. 13-14.

Over time, the Catalan nationalist movement's EU strategy has become more moderate in practice. While nationalist rhetoric emphasises the recognition of Catalonia as a "nation" within Europe, in practice this strategy is distinctly more regionalist in nature. The demands for increased participation in EU matters have focused on improving institutionalised mechanisms of co-operation through both the Sectoral Conferences and bilateral relations. Accordingly the measures demanded include:

1. full co-operation and increased two-way flow of information in Community processes;

2. co-responsibility in the decision-making processes;

3. the presence of the autonomous communities in the Spanish delegations, EU institutions and the COREPER;

4. institutional recognition of the EU's existing plurinational character;

5. recognition of the right of the autonomous communities to maintain a foreign policy of a cultural and commercial nature;

6. the establishment of mechanisms for the active participation of the autonomous communities in the composition, demand and distribution of structural and cohesion funds.

The achievements in addressing the issue of participatory rights for Catalonia and the other Spanish autonomous communities in EU matters have not yet resolved the conflict between: 1) those who argue that only the central government can represent the Spanish state in its entirety in EU matters and 2) those that who believe that only sub-national authorities can represent the differing cultures and nationalities co-existing within the Spanish state. Nevertheless, the achievements have certainly helped overcome some of the obstacles. Like the process of European integration, the process of consolidating sub-national participation will require a constant search for consensus. Otherwise, the Spanish position in Brussels may find itself weakened by the constant conflict within the Spanish state. If the Spanish state's representation abroad is not to be undermined, it is crucial that the autonomous communities participate in elaborating the position of the Spanish government in the EU and in applying EU legislation. By institutionalising the participatory rights of the autonomous communities, both in practical and constitutional terms, the key role of sub-national authorities in the Spanish state will be recognised.

Europe à la carte and Autonomy à la carte

Over the last few decades, it has become increasingly clear that the processes of regionalisation and European integration have had significant effects on the nature and role of the nation-state. The case of Catalonia illustrates that sub-national authorities are unlikely to form an alternative to the traditional nation-state. Catalonia relies on the same sources of law, the international economic order and collective security relied upon by the Spanish state. However, what is occurring is a shift away from the nation-state as a central unit of analysis when describing political systems in Western Europe. There is a growing recognition of the weaknesses of the nation-state while it is acknowledged that the state will not disappear. In functional terms, its role as a mediator or filter continues to be important. Nevertheless, it will need to adapt to the pluralism of modern society be it from below or from above.

The Catalan case clearly demonstrates how these twin processes have evolved simultaneously with significant legal-constitutional, political and sociological implications. Examples of policy areas in which the Catalan government has effectively asserted its objectives at a European level by succeeding in bypassing the national level, have begun to emerge[2].

Specifically however, the Catalan case has generated some interesting conclusions. Most importantly, the Catalan nationalist movement has employed a regionalist strategy for nationalist objectives in the area of European integration. After a period of initial enthusiasm in the late 1980s and first half of the 1990s, Catalan nationalists have opted for a dual strategy, co-operating with the central government while maintaining active participation in EU institutions. This policy has been aided by the

---

[2]   One example would the Catalan government's successful attempt in November 1997 at persuading the Commission to initiate legislation regarding the labeling of products in the other 'co-official' languages of Spain: Catalan, Basque and Galician. Along the same lines and coinciding with the Commission's consideration of the Generalitat's initiative, the controversial law of the Catalan language was being debated in the European Parliament, a move initiated by the Spanish government (See El País, 7 November, 1997).

pragmatic nature of the nationalist movement, with roots in a tradition of modernising the political and economic structures of the Spanish state. This tradition is also reflected in the movement's participation within the Spanish State of Autonomies. Thus, the impact of the process of European integration on sub-national politics must be taken into account within the broader context of democratic consolidation, economic modernisation and the institutionalisation of new types of political structures and frameworks. It is therefore important to contextualise European integration as one of several variables and particularly, its evolving nature.

The consolidation of the Spanish State of Autonomies is occurring simultaneously with the process of European integration. The Europeanisation of the Catalan nationalist movement has developed exposed by these two processes. Recent years, however, have seen growing divisions within the Catalan political party system on the question of Europe, specifically with regards to Catalonia's role in it. Domestic considerations have led Catalan nationalists to turn away from the Committee of the Regions as a viable institution within which their demands at the European level can be articulated. Indeed, they have managed to establish a direct line of communication to Madrid and from there to Brussels while maintaining a myriad of links with other Spanish and EU sub-national authorities. Where this strategy will lead is difficult to determine but nonetheless raises the importance of the issues of regionalisation and European integration as part of a new political agenda within Catalonia, Spain, and the European Union. In terms of further research, it would be interesting to see whether the Catalan example has generated a "spill-over" effect for other Spanish or EU regions. Many see the Catalan case as the model to follow. Its permanence and stability as a strategy is key for other sub-national authorities to take the initiative and follow suit. From a normative point of view, there is clear need to develop new conceptual frameworks to explain the concurrent development of supranationalism and new forms of nationalism, adjusting to new institutional and constitutional frameworks. This type of nationalism no longer requires the construction of a nation-state to obtain autonomy and instead seeks to promote a new form of non-territorial form of public recognition in new boundary-free multicultural space at the supranational level.

References:

Díez Medrano, Juan (1995). Divided Nations: Class, Politics, and Nationalism in the Basque Country and Catalonia, Ithaca: Cornell University Press.

Sharpe, L.J. (1988) "The growth and decentralization of the modern democratic state," *European Journal of Political Research*, 16 (3).

Wilson, Thomas M. and Smith, M. Estellie (1993). *Cultural Change and the New Europe*, Boulder: Westview Press, Inc.

2000/2001

GOVERNING EUROPE: WHAT ROLE FOR THE REGIONS AND CITIES IN THE EU?

Chairman of the jury

Prof. Kurt Schelter (DE), Minister for Justice and European Affairs of the Land Brandenburg

Theses submitted

NUMBER OF ENTRANTS	LANGUAGES		COUNTRY	
25	7	German English Spanish French Italian Dutch Portuguese	12	Austria Belgium Denmark Spain France Greece Ireland Italy Latvia Netherlands Portugal United Kingdom

Winners:

First prize:

Dr Romain Pasquier (FR), *The political capacity of regions. A comparison of France and Spain*, University of Rennes I

Second prize:

Dr Rob Schobben (NL), *Political regions and the European Union*, University of Twente

First special mention:

Dr Laura L. Huici Sancho (ES) *The role of the Committee of the Regions in the European Integration Process*, University of Barcelona

Second special mention:

Dr Stefaan De Rynck (BE), *The politics of change: Education and environmental policy in the Belgian communities and regions*, European University Institute, Florence

Romain Pasquier, University of Rennes I

The political capacity of regions. A comparison of France and Spain

Regional political capacity in a polycentric Europe

The combination of forces of devolution, European integration and economic globalisation has made the recomposition of nation states one of the most important questions facing contemporary political scientists. Many observers consider that the political forces of devolution and Community integration, combined with the dynamics of economic globalisation, call into question the legitimacy of the action of central administrations. Several factors could explain the loss of the central role of the state (Wright and Cassese 1996): the crisis in the welfare state; the ideological crisis following the swing towards neoliberalism; internationalisation of the economy; and the progress of European integration and of devolution. In Western Europe, until the 1960s, the legitimacy of the State was based on its ability to ensure economic development by means of massive state intervention, and gradually to reduce social inequalities by redistributing the wealth that had been created. This equation legitimising the Keynesian welfare state has been blown out of the water in that the type of political regulation on which it was based has been eroded, i.e. the territorial control by state authority of a society and an economy integrated within the national territory (Badie 1995). New sub-national and supranational political entities are emerging. There is no longer a single power centre with the resources needed to resolve collective problems (Mayntz 1993). This erosion of state control is all the more noticeable given that the social conditions within which State services operate have also changed significantly due to the decline in the great social intermediaries of the post-war years: the Church, trade unions, and political parties. New political demands emerged during the 1970s and 80s due to the changes in the labour market and the promotion of values known as post-materialist, such as respect for the environment or cultural identities. These values generate new kinds of social movements whose demands are far removed from traditional concerns. These new interests escape the centralised, sectoral control of central governments that came about during the thirty "glorious years" following the Second World War.

It is now time to start thinking about new ways of doing politics. One hypothesis is the new relevance of sub-national political arrangements. Polycentric political stages and actors would create dynamics affecting the landscape of interests, identities, public action and economic development (Balme, 1996; Le Galès 2003). The possible strengthening of the role of the regions is a key dimension to this process, as it is these that appear to provide a focus for interests, identities and public action. Devolution policies carried out by various European countries over the last thirty years give them increasing political resources. Moreover, the creation of a European political space expands their scope for action significantly. Regions enter into direct discussions with the European Commission and play a role in the implementation of European public policy. Are the regions taking advantage of this new scope for action? Are they emerging as new spaces for political power?

The theoretical framework: regional political capacity

Debates about this question go way beyond academic research, and often come to contradictory conclusions. Behind the myth of the "Europe of regions", the true picture is a kaleidoscope of institutional and political structures[1]. The functions carried out by regional-level administrations in Germany, Austria, Belgium, Spain, France and Italy differ quite significantly. Devolution policies are far from being consistent within the European Union. Whilst the United Kingdom has recently created regional parliaments in Scotland and Wales, Finland, Greece, Ireland and Portugal do not have regional structures for political representation or the implementation of public policy. As for the countries of central Europe that are preparing to join the EU, such as Poland and the Czech Republic, regionalisation is pending on national policy agendas, but no significant reform has yet been carried out. We should add that the regionalisation of political interaction and public action at European level has had mixed, indeed contradictory reviews depending on the country, the region and the sector (Jeffery 1997; Keating and Loughlin 1997; Le Galès and Lequesne 1997; Négrier and Jouve 1998).

Thus, numerous researchers agree that the mobilising potential of the regions varies considerably. A combination of institutional, political or cultural factors are often

---

[1]   This difficulty faced the Statistical Office of the European Communities when measuring territorial disparities. It was forced to distinguish between three types of territorial statistical units (NUTS I, NUTS II, NUTS III) in order to cover the variety of "regional" levels in Europe, from the German *Länder* to the British counties.

cited to account for these differences. However, political sociology lacks more systematic and convincing interpretational frameworks. My thesis therefore offers a sociological interpretation of the variations in the mobilising potential of the regions in Europe, based on a comparative analysis of the *political capacity* of the regions in France and Spain (Pasquier, 2004). Political capacity is derived from the notion of "capacity to govern" (Stone 1989) and can be defined as a complex process of defining interests and organising and coordinating collective action that enables institutions and groups of public and/or private-sector actors to address collective problems within the regions, which are characterised by fragmented and flexible forms of action. Political capacity is not, therefore, simply a matter of institutional resources, but leads to the creation of forms of cooperation between institutions and various actors in response to perceived challenges. This does not mean that there is no conflict in socio-political relations, but that the process of government needs practices and standards that affect the capacity for collective action and political regulation of regional institutions and actors. The hypothesis being defended here is that regions' political capacity is part of a bigger picture involving rules, practices and beliefs that have built up over time on the regional and national scale, and which facilitate or limit their scope for action and political regulation. This slow process of building up practices, rules and beliefs over the long history of relations between the centre and outlying areas, at regional and national level, is where the explanation of variations in regional political capacity must be sought.

Thus, the analysis is first of all focussed on the construction of *regional models of collective action.* These can be defined as a collection of political practices and attitudes that have been built up and territorialised over time, and which direct the logic behind the actions of groups of regional players. These models of collective action vary greatly from region to region. Regions evoke memories and identities that are part of their specific history, and have different political structures and relations with the state. Regional institutions were not created out of thin air. They are the result of a combination of institutional and socio-political dynamics that has given rise to configurations of actors and cognitive frameworks that vary greatly from region to region. Some owe their institutional existence only to administrative reforms imposed by the central government, whilst others formed as spaces for collective mobilisation long before their existence was recognised in law. Institutions are characterised by specific modes of collective action resulting from their history and the practices and attitudes of the players and social groups which sustain them. This constitutes a cognitive and normative basis for action.

The *national styles of local and regional politics* are another variable that is key to the understanding of the makeup of a region's political capacity. These national styles determine all the institutional rules and resources as well as the public policy procedures that shape relations between regions and central governments (Richardson *et al* 1982). By sharing out various levels of political resources, by determining the size and shape of regions, by defining the procedures of negotiation, formulation and implementation of public policy, these styles determine the national frameworks for action into which the strategies of regional players fit. Having settled over time, they play a part in defining the relationships between levels of administration and heavily influence the development of regional capacity.

Regions are involved in a wide range of public activities. Whether at national or Community level, the major challenges of public policy are managed through processes that involve several levels of administration and give rise to a highly complex set of inter-institutional relationships. The realisation of political capacity is analysed from two perspectives: the capacity of regions to build coalitions around the major issues of regional development, and the capacity they have to implement policy measures to resolve a number of collective problems. Regions need to be capable of negotiating with several levels of government on a number of public policy issues at national and European level. They need to build coalitions (local authorities, socio-occupational groups), become a spokesperson for their area, and represent its interests in various external public policy arenas. Regions can thus become the geographical expression of "issue coalitions", addressing certain political and/or public policy challenges (Sabatier 1998). The other dimension of regional political capacity is the formulation of public policy. Over the last twenty years, the responsibility for dealing with a whole series of problems has been devolved. Certain collective problems (economic development, environment, culture) can now be dealt with at regional level through regional public policy mechanisms. Regions are now in a position to play a significant role in local governance.

The key results of a comparative research strategy

We have attempted to put this theoretical framework into practice by means of a study comparing France and Spain. Our investigations involved two French regions and two Spanish ones: Brittany and the Centre region in France, and Galicia and La Rioja in Spain. Choosing two regions per country makes it possible to develop a comparison on two levels – international and inter-regional – and thus to go beyond the traditional contrasting of national political systems. The choice of countries is based on the fact that France and Spain have enough in common to make a comparison possible. Until the end of the 1970s/beginning of the 1980s, France and Spain were both centralised, unitary states that had very similar models of public administration and territorial organisation, which were heavily influenced by the Napoleonic model. Moreover, the French and Spanish central governments almost simultaneously began regional government reforms that, at the beginning of the 1980s, led to the creation of regional institutions elected by direct universal suffrage. Finally, as Member States of the European Union, these countries are involved in the development of European public policy. The analysis of the complex relationships between regionalisation and Europeanisation is thus made easier. The choice of regions within these countries reflects a priority of selecting, as far as possible, little-studied regions that have followed very distinct socio-political paths. Recent analyses of the dynamics of regionalisation in Europe have often drawn on the symbolic but now clichéd cases of Catalonia in Spain, Rhône Alpes in France, Baden-Württemberg in Germany, or Tuscany in Italy. The chosen regions have been the subject or little, if any, of the recent research on regional governance, and have very different histories within their countries whilst nonetheless having certain similarities between the two countries. Thus, Brittany and Galicia have seen groups of actors on a regional scale coming into play since the end of the 19th century, whereas the Centre region and La Rioja have developed more recently as a direct result of the devolution process in France and Spain.

This comparative study emphasises that changes in the inter-organisational environment of the European regions should not hide the heterogeneity of their political capacity, i.e. their capacity to regionalise a series of collective problems (economic development, environment, spatial planning, research, transport, universities, education, public health, and culture). This study develops a diachronic interpretation of this diversity. This slow process of building up practices, rules and beliefs over the long history of relations between the centre and outlying areas, at regional and national level, is where the explanation of variations in regional political capacity must be sought. Two variables weigh heavily on regional political capacity: the models of collective action that they have developed over the course of their history and, following on from that, the national styles of territorial public action into which they fit. The prevalence of these regional models of collective action can be identified at several stages in this research in terms of the informal modes of negotiations between the regional elites and the central government, the capacity of regional institutions to become the legitimate voice of the region, in the perception and the mobilisation of the French and Spanish regions in the face of European issues, and again in the methods of implementing regional public policy as shown by the example of local development. National styles of territorial policy, for their part, determine the level of institutional resources, establish the rules that help build the regional political markets, and set procedures for coordinating the actions of central governments and those of the regions. Neither the length of standing of mobilisations nor the extent of institutional resources allow us to make any presumptions about modes of collective action or about regional political capacity. Regions with strong regional identities can prove to be highly fragmented and divided political spaces (Pasquier 2003). Conversely, regions that do not on the face of it have a clearly visible potential for identity can emerge as new spaces for political problem-solving, for example as a result of external dynamics. The historical inheritance of practices and cognitive frameworks, of institutions, of interest structures, and of public policy mechanisms, has both a constraining and an enabling effect on the scope for action of regional institutions.

On an analytical level, it is possible to distinguish between two dimensions in the exercise of this political capacity: the capacity to bring together coalitions of local interests in the context of multi-level action, and the capacity to produce regionalised public policy mechanisms. This is a fundamental distinction, as it makes it possible to move away from a exclusively institutionalist vision of regional mobilisations. The experience of CELIB in France in the 1950s and 60s or of Catalan employers at the beginning of the 20th century clearly shows that territorial political capacity can be built up through informal coalitions of groups of social, political or economic actors. The formal existence of a regional institution that supposedly embodies an area does not automatically give rise to a real capacity to regulate or to represent the interests of the region across a range of political issues.

With regard to the first aspect, the capacity to defend the interests of the region at multiple levels, analysis shows that only a few regions are capable of producing sustainable coalitions to defend the region's interests. Galicia and Brittany have the most structured coalitions. In Brittany, the early learning of collective bargaining and the relative consensus of the political and economic elite on key issues of economic development is a resource that is key to the way the region is currently run. The regional council is able to bring together a coalition of a wide range of sub-regional networks (local authorities, chambers of commerce) around a vision of regional development. The example of Brittany demonstrates a regional political capacity where the regional council plays the role of spokesperson of a broader territorial coalition when dealing with the central government and the European Commission. In Galicia, regional capacity is even greater, to the extent that the elites who share the desire to defend a wide-ranging political autonomy and the desire to break with the image of an under-developed Galicia draw on a significant level of institutional resources and a highly regionalised political environment. The regional government has a monopoly on representing regional interests, whether at national or European level. In the Centre region, on the other hand, the regional council is faced with highly fragmented networks of sub-regional actors and very limited legitimacy of the regional space. This context severely limits the institution's capacity to form coalitions of actors in a forward-looking environment, whether during negotiations of the CPER (State-Region Contract Plan) or the allocation of the Structural Funds. The position of La Rioja is somewhere between the two, but the trend is towards developing an increasing political capacity. The regional elites are developing a form of economic neo-regionalism linked to the Basque government's "aggressive" fiscal policy. Its scope for action is constrained by the limited influence that the political regional elite has at the central level, in particular within the large networks of the main political parties, the PSOE and the PP. However, in recent years, it has extended to the European level, with the regional government being increasingly active on issues relating to the vital economic interests of this region (wine-growing).

On the second aspect, regulatory capacity through public policy mechanisms, the example of territorial development policy shows that, in the French and Spanish regions, regional public policy networks are coming into existence and are passing on their own principles for action to local actors. In the area of local development, these regions are at the heart of the major changes in regional governance. More specifically, French and German regional elites are revamping the framework of their relations with local actors by promoting the supra-municipal space (*pays* and *comarca*) in order to establish a partnership with the local political and economic elites. The impact of these policies can be evaluated in terms of the institutional conflicts they generate. They come up against more traditional forms of political negotiation controlled by the general councils and provincial governments. Thus, indirectly, regional governance helps to change the conditions in which territorial power, and more broadly that of local government, is exercised. However, depending on the regional or national context, the intensity and the effects of these policies vary. In Brittany, despite the weakness of regional institutions, this policy has significant structural effects as a result of the practices of stronger cooperation between institutions and groups of public and private-sector actors in the region. Conversely, in the Centre region and in Galicia, regional administrations are faced with strong opposition from general councils and provincial governments, which do not want to lose their political power. Furthermore, the direction of the changes generated by these policies is heavily influenced by national channels: the French and Spanish central governments are trying in different ways to maintain their influence over regional governance.

More generally, it would appear that regional political capacity is taking on more institutionalised, and therefore more stable, forms in Spain than in France. In Spain, the volume of institutional resources held by the autonomous communities, and the greater autonomy of regional political markets, significantly influence the strategic position of regional governments within the networks of actors. The autonomisation of regional political markets is an important dynamic, as it contributes to the territorialisation of political issues into the regional space, and thus interacts with the building of regional interests and on the interest of social groups and of elites in taking action on issues of specific interest. In this respect, the Spanish regions, though unequally structured, function broadly around the issue of defending and promoting regional interests based on the presence of a regionalist and/or nationalist party. This autonomisation of regional political markets raises the profile of regional debates in political competition. Regional governments, at the centre of these political markets, have a virtual monopoly on representation to the outside world. Thus, the Spanish autonomous communities are in a very real sense intermediate governments, meso-governments, whose activities are directed towards satisfying the interests and the social identities of the sub-national groups they represent.

In France, there is no real regional political space to speak of[2], but there are regional spaces that are to varying degrees sensitive to regional issues. In this respect, the Centre region is an extreme example of non-regionalisation of issues. Since this region was created, it has not been the reference point for local elites. Brittany is a less extreme case. A regional political space certainly exists, in which regional debates take shape and where collective macro-representations of the region and its problems are produced. This awareness among large sections of society of regional themes makes it easier for the regional elites to mobilise people. However, in France, regional councils must coexist with a collection of sub-regional institutions, which have equivalent legal and financial resources at their disposal. Thus, the political capacity of the French regions will depend on their ability to integrate, i.e. the institution's capacity to play the role of regional spokesman by building cooperation between a variety of public and private players on the basis of jointly-defined regional interests. Institutional and financial resources contribute to this ability to integrate, but there are other dimensions, such as the capacity to represent the region in a way that inspires and embodies the regional community. In Brittany, the regional institution has this capacity to bring about strong cooperation between regional actors around specific interests and to draw up a common strategy, whatever the issue may be. In the Centre region, on the other hand, the regional council's ability to integrate is particularly limited, largely because the general councils and the cities are opposed to this regionalisation of relationships. Thus, if regional political capacity is increasing in France, this is due to the emergence or the consolidation of coalitions of a variety of networks of actors, of which the regional institution is merely the spokesman. This is particularly clear when it comes to the allocation of the Structural Funds, the policies of inter-regional cooperation.

Conclusion

This diachronic interpretation of political capacity does not, however, confirm the idea that regions' scope for action is somehow inherent. The short-term view taken by many research projects on regional mobilisation has often tended to over-emphasise the changes in regional strategies in the 1980s and 1990s, when in fact these have taken place over a much longer period. This publication invites the reader to think about the changes by measuring them against the pre-existing national and regional socio-political contexts. The creation of a European political space has effects on the

---

[2]   With the possible exception of Corsica.

representations and practices of regional elites. However, the changes are incremental, more diffuse and less linear than they appear. An analysis of the allocation of the Structural Funds, for example, highlights the importance of the national styles of regional policy. The management of these funds does not fundamentally change the structure of relations between central governments and the regions. On the contrary, it reproduces political relationships that are rooted in French-style contractualisation or non-cooperative federalism in Spain. On the other hand, the study of regional local development policies or of inter-regional cooperation policies highlights the fact that the regions' scope for actions develops along rather roundabout routes. The regions that have benefited from Community programmes over the years are reappropriating them to produce regionalised mechanisms in the organisation of local areas. Moreover, the portfolio of regional leaders is extending to European level as the scope of the Union's competencies widens. The number of issues requiring political solutions is increasing, and certain regional authorities are adapting to this, for example by increasing inter-regional cooperation, as shown by the examples of Brittany and the Pays de la Loire, and by Galicia and the region of North Portugal. The French and Spanish regions are thus taking part in a process of bottom-up Europeanisation.

Change cannot, therefore, be taken for granted, as multi-level governance theorists would all too often have us believe. Some regions seem to have more predispositions than others. Paradoxically, the construction of a polycentric world of action gives more value to regional models of collective action. Regions that have specific identities and unique collective practices are better able to position themselves in these inter-organisational exchanges and in the new political networks that are coming together at European level. In this new context, it is necessary to have interests to defend, which presupposes a common identity and scope for action.

References:

Balme R., ed., *Les politiques du néo-régionalisme*, Economica, Paris, 1996.

Badie B., *La fin des territoires*, Fayard, Paris, 1995.

Jeffery C., ed., *The Regional Dimension of the European Union. Toward a third level in Europe?*, Franck Cass, London, 1997.

Keating M., Loughlin J., eds, *The Political Economy of Regionalism*, Franck Cass, London, 1996.

Le Galès P., *Le retour des villes en Europe*, Presses de Sciences Po, Paris, 2003.

Le Galès P., Lequesne C., eds., *Les paradoxes des régions en Europe*, La Découverte, Paris, 1997.

Mayntz R., *Governing failures and the Problem of Governability : Some Comments on a Theoretical Paradigm*, in Kooiman J., ed., *Modern Governance*, Sage, London, 1993.

Négrier E., Jouve B., dir., *Que gouvernent les régions d'Europe? Echanges politiques et mobilisations sub-nationales*, L'Harmattan, Paris, 1998.

Pasquier R., *La capacité politique des régions. Une comparaison France/Espagne*, Preface by Yves Mény, Presses universitaires de Rennes, Rennes, 2004.

Pasquier R., *From Patterns of Collective Action to the Capacity for Governance in French Regions*, in Bukowski J., Piattoni S., Smyrl M., eds., *Between Global Economy and Local Society : Political Actors and Territorial Governance*, Lanham, MD Rowman and Littlefield, 2003.

Richardson J., Gustafsson G., Jordan G., *The Concept of Policy Style*, in Richardson J., ed., *Policy Styles in Western Europe*, George Allen & Unwin, London, 1982.

Sabatier P., 1998, *The Advocacy Coalition framework : Revisions and Relevance for Europe*, *Journal of European Public Policy*, 5, (1).

Stone C., *Regime Politics, Governing Atlanta*, University Press of Kansas, Lawrence, 1989.

Wright V., Cassese S., eds., *La recomposition de l'Etat en Europe*, La Découverte, Paris, 1996.

Rob Schobben, University of Twente

Political regions and the European Union

This study deals with regions in Europe. The combination is not arbitrary. Given the contemporary politico-institutional situation in the European Union, of which regional units form part, it is impossible to confine the study of regions to the limited context of the nation-state. The connections between regions and the European institutional setting reveal themselves in various ways. The European, nation and regional levels are inextricably bound up with each other.

The aim of this study is to gain insight into the role political regions play and can play in the European context. The central research question is:

What is the present role of political regions in the (member-states of the) European Union and what future role can they play?

The part of the central research question concerning the present role of political regions is elaborated in three more specific research questions that are successively dealt with in chapters two, three and four.

In *chapter two* attention is paid to the concept "region". The research question is:

What does the term "region" mean and what are the meanings of the related terms "regionalisation" and "regionalism"?

The concept "region" can be analysed in various manners. A main distinction is that between *single feature region* and *multiple feature region*. The first term designates regions that are identified on the basis of one distinctive characteristic, for instance, an economic, historic or functional one. The second term signifies more comprehensive regions in which various dimensions are combined. The analysis in this chapter leads to the choice of the concept "political region" as the main object of the rest of this study. A "political region" is:

A territorial unit, forming part of a larger whole, either located on the territory of one state or on those of more states, in which – on the basis of authentic communal solidarity – a human community exists, that devotes itself to the promotion of the interests of its members, in a relatively autonomous democratically legitimised organizational form that operates within conditions set by higher authorities.

Political regions are often at the intersection of two distinct but related processes: regionalisation and regionalism. Regionalisation is a process resulting in regional governmental arrangements serving to fulfil functional and planning tasks. Regionalism rests on ideologies or is embodied in political movements that are supported by the population of certain regions. Regionalisation and regionalism may coincide but this need not be the case. The distinction between regionalisation and regionalism reflects the tensions between the ideas associated with functionalism, territorialism and (cultural) identity. In terms of identity on the one hand and territoriality on the other, a ascending line can be drawn from regional areas lacking autonomy (deconcentrated areas), via areas possessing little autonomy (functional regionalisation), through areas with higher degree of autonomy (political regionalism) to areas with the highest possible degree of regional autonomy (federated states within a federation).

There is a gradual difference between regionalism and nationalism. Both are concerned with the collective expression of the unitedness of a particular population. Each nation is identified in terms of a people. When nation, people and state coincide, a sovereign nation-state emerges. Analogously, one can say that a political region emerges in case a regional population is governed by a regional authority with a high degree of autonomy.

The research question of *chapter three* is:

What is the present relationship between political regions and the European Union?

A distinction is made between a *formal*, an *informal* and a *material* relationship between the EU and the political regions.

First, the role of the subsidiarity principle with respect to the *formal, institutionalised* relationship is examined. Traditionally, this principle requires the exercise of authority to take place at the lowest possible level. At present, the situation in the EU differs from this ideal. Under the current treaty provision (article 5 EC), the principle is restricted to the relation between the member-states and the EU. This is striking given the history of the principle, in which the role of lower government levels has always been put first. The second formal relation between the EU and political regions manifests itself in the role of the Committee of the Regions in EU decision-making processes. It is very important that there exists such an interest-promoting organ for subnational governments within the EU. The position of the Committee of the Regions is not comparable, however, to the position of the institutions of the EU. Certain institutional adjustments could help the Committee to achieve a more powerful position. For the short term, one might think of recognizing the Committee also as an EU institution. Furthermore, a right of appeal to the Court of Justice and a political mandate for the members of the Committee could help to improve the Committee's position. In the long term, the Committee could be transformed into a genuine representational body of regional (and local) governments in the EU. An adequate regulation of the formal relations between the political regions and the EU does not have to mean that existent *informal relations* between th EU and the regional governments would have to be severed. Supplementary to the Committee's functioning as a formal organ or an institution, there is enough space left for informal interest-promoting activities aof umbrella-organizations and Regional Offices.

The material relations between the EU and the political regions mainly concern the flows of money coming from the structural funds of the EU. Over the years it has become clear that the partners are dependent on each other for realising more effective and efficient regional policies. The idea of co-operation has been woven into the structural policy regulations. The principles forming the bases of the structural funds regulations lead to situations in which all parties involved, whether public or private, have to co-operate to reach an optimal result. This means that in all phases of the policy cycle the promotion of European, national, regional and local interests has to be co-ordinated.

The European Union is integrating at a high pace. Yet, in many areas there still remain high barriers for regional governments to co-operate across state borders. Nation-states remain the masters of their own internal organisation; they determine their own territorial authorities enjoy autonomy. This leads to numerous co-ordination problems. In *chapter four* attention is paid to the forms in which political regions can so-operate across national borders. The research question is:

What forms of cross-border interregional co-operation can be distinguished?

Although international law enables decentral governments to co-operate across national borders, the extent of this form of cross-border co-operation is limited. Existing transfrontier authorities in the European Union still wrestle with problems caused by barriers put up on the basis of the idea of national sovereignty. So far, political regions across borders do not exist. In order to achieve more integration such bodies ought to be created. This would also prepare the grounds for a direct relation between cross-border political regions and the European Union. The population of such regions could be given the right to elect autonomous euregional councils. Obviously, this requires mutual adjustments between the tasks and competences of the cross-border authorities and those of nationsl decentral authorities.

Chapter five is dedicated to a comparison of the political regions in the member-states of the European Union. The research question is:

How are the regional governments in the countries of the European Union constituted and what similarities and differences reveal themselves?

In the first place, attention is paid to the constitutional structures of member-states and the room they make for political regions. With regard to constitutional structures the spectrum runs from centralistic unitarian states, via decentralized unitarian states, and regionalized states, to federal states. Obviously, the positions of regions within these structures are different. In some cases one cannot even speak of the existence of political regions (Portugal and Luxemburg), while in other cases there are only poorly developed political regions (Greece, Great Britain, Ireland and Finland). In yet other member-states political regions enjoy a certain degree of autonomy (France, The Netherlands, Denmark, Sweden). In regionalized states (Italy, Spain, Belgium) the political tegions have a firm autonomous position that is, as a rule, constitutionally guaranteed. Finally, federated states enjoy the highest possible degree of autonomy (Germany and Austria).

These differences in position of political regions in the member-states of the European Union is reflected in their capacities to co-operate autonomously across state borders. The stronger political regions are, the more possibilities they have to work together across borders. The French, Dutch and Swedish decentral governments are capable of co-operation across borders within their own domains of competence. However, the primary responsibility for foreign relations remains with the central governments. The Belgian regions and communities, as well as the German and Austrian *Länder* even possess treaty making capacities within their own legislative and regulative competence's.

The current positions of political regions in the European Union are diverse. Differences in national positions determine the relationships between political regions and the European Union. They are also of importance where the participation of political regions in interest-promoting organisations, in the Committee of the Regions or in cross-border co-operation is concerned.

In order to give indications about the future role of the political regions in the European Union, one has to investigate changing relations between the political regions and the member-states, as well as between the political regions and the European Union. This requires a better understanding of the future of the European integration in general, which is the central theme of chapter six. The research question is:

What visions on European integration do exist and to what extent is there a place for political regions in them?

The intergovernmental relations within the European Union become more and more complex. As an illustration of such processes, the structural policy of the European Union is sketched. The example makes clear that there are no uniform relations between the European Union, the member-states and political regions. The special features of the Policy fields, the attitudes of the member-states, and the institutional positions of the political regions all have their particular influence. European integration theories point into different directions in which the European Union might evolve. In *chapter six* a number of integration theories and the roles for political regions they allow for are reviewed. The extreme positions on the scale are occupied by the intergovernmental view, in which states are seen as "Lords of the Treaties" on the one hand and the federalist view, in which the Unites States of Europe form the end-scenario, on the other. Further, attention is paid to a great variety of ideas concerning forms of differentiated integration that have been proposed. Differentiated integration opens space for co-existent forms of limited co-operation. Such scenarios offer instruments to avoid forms of comprehensive integration without running the risk of total stagnation. On the other hand, differentiated integration runs counter to the idea of a unified Europe.

Integration theories lead to the question what model of the future European Union will guarantee the most favourable conditions for the development of relatively independent political regions. In chapter seven, various models for the future development of the European Union are considered in light of the assumption that they should be capable of ascribing a role of some importance to political regions. The research question is:

What institutional developments of the European Union are conceivable and which of them is optimal from the viewpoint of the political regions?

It is shown that the most favourable option for political regions is a development towards double federalisation. The final outcome of such a process will be a federal Europe consisting of member states that are in their turn federal in character, with the political regions as their constituent elements. This model offers the best prospects for political regions to preserve their own identity as well as a high degree of autonomy.

From the viewpoint of the principle of subsidiarity this is an attractive model as well. Catalogues of guaranteed regulative and governmental competence's for political regions, member-states and the European Union will have to be included in a European Constitution. A Constitutional Court ought to supervise compliance with the principle and with the division of competence's following from the catalogues. When the contours of a competence do not follow clearly from the catalogues, appeal should be made to an adapted principle of subsidiarity. This principle reads as follows:

In areas which do not fall within its exclusive competence, the Community shall take action, in accordance with the principle of subsidiarity, only if and insofar as the objectives if the proposed action cannot be sufficiently achieved by the Member States and the political regions and can therefore, by reason of scale or effects of the proposed action, be better achieved by the Community.

Provision should be made for a proportional representation of political regions in a "Third Chamber" of the European Parliament.

It was not intended to sketch the future model of the European Union. The objective was to sketch the optimal model from the viewpoint of the political regions. It is obvious that in the long run important institutional choices have to be made. One of the possible scenarios, in which the political regions are formally acknowledged as territorial units based on cultural identity and with rights to look after their own interests in an eventual building blocks of a new political order of the European Union. The problems of the division of political and administrative competence's within the EU amounts to striking the right balance between the various governmental layers. Given the opposite processes of europeanisation on the one hand and regionalisation and decentralisation on the other, an intergovernmental or even a neo-functional model of integration is no longer feasible. A classical federal model, however, would put too much focus on the relationship between the EU and the nation-states.

The advantage of a model of double federalisation is, while the requisite competence of EU organs for the Union to be able to operate in the international plane is guaranteed, it also respects the position of the present nation-states. The nation-states can keep the grater part of their actual "sovereign" competence's. At the same time, there is room for the political regions to develop themselves into important players in EU decision-making processes. In this way, the involvement of citizens in EU decision-making can be improved. A model of double federalisation is an alternative that should be seriously considered with a view to the future revision of the European institutional design.

Laura L. Huici Sancho, University of Barcelona

The role of the Committee of the Regions in the process of European integration

1.   Introduction

The process of European integration is a unique phenomenon. From the point of view of international public law, the European Community is clearly an international organisation to which its Member States have increasingly transferred specific sovereign powers in central internal and external policy areas. Against this background, in the light of the debate on the new Treaty establishing a Constitution for Europe, it is worth considering the institutional structure of the European Union.

Since its creation with the Maastricht Treaty of 1992, the role of the Committee of the Regions in the process of European integration has slowly but surely become more concrete. The reforms made in the Treaties of Amsterdam and Nice made significant changes to those provisions of the Treaty establishing the European Community relating to the Committee. More specifically, the Amsterdam Treaty revoked the protocol establishing a common organisational structure with the Economic and Social Committee, thus granting greater autonomy to the Committee of the Regions, as well as giving it the power to approve its own internal Rules of Procedure. The Treaty of Nice responded to the Committee's request that its members be required to be elected representatives "who either hold a regional or local authority electoral mandate or are politically accountable to an elected assembly", thus confirming its status as a political body representing constituent elements of the institutional and territorial structures of the Member States that are nonetheless independent of their central governments.

The text of the draft Constitutional Treaty approved by the Convention on the Future of Europe contains a further series of amendments that significantly strengthen the position of the Committee of the Regions. For example, it has at last been expressly granted the right to institute proceedings before the Court of Justice with the aim of annulling acts that infringe its prerogatives or, more importantly, upholding the subsidiarity principle. The Committee's role in ensuring that this principle is correctly applied has also been recognised, although it is only able to refer to the Court of Justice in this respect on matters on which it must be consulted. The draft does not, however, take account of other proposals submitted by the Committee of the Regions. It is neither recognised as an institution nor granted the power of co-decision in specific areas, e.g. those connected with cross-border cooperation, nor is it awarded the right to submit oral and written questions to the Commission. Moreover, the European institutions are not bound by the draft Treaty to state their reasons for not taking account of opinions issued by the Committee of the Regions, a change the latter has been pushing for since its very beginnings.

Some of these proposals may seem surprising at first glance. However, when analysed in detail, the position of the Committee throughout the successive Treaty reforms tallies with a clear philosophy, i.e. to make the Committee of the Regions the third pillar of the democratic legitimacy of the European Union, together with the European Council and Parliament. Is this overly ambitious?" Taking account of the fact that the Committee is currently a purely consultative body, which, furthermore, is required to be consulted on a smaller range of issues than the Economic and Social Committee (despite progress made through the successive reforms), then it would appear that it almost certainly is. However, when considering the role of the Committee of the Regions for the future of Europe, it is necessary to look at issues that go beyond the role currently attributed to it by the Treaties. Rather, the function carried out by this body within the process of European integration must be taken into account. This function is determined above all by two sets of opposing forces that characterise this process: the principle of effectiveness versus that of democratic legitimacy; and unity versus diversity. Against the backdrop of this twofold tension the Committee of the Regions does indeed play a quite specific and essential role in achieving the priority objective of closeness to the citizen, which is decisive in ensuring the process of European integration makes sound progress.

2. Contribution to the effectiveness and democratic legitimacy of the European Union

The Committee of the Regions was created by the Intergovernmental Conference of 1991 with the aim of reducing the democratic deficit of the process of European integration. The Committee of the Regions came into being in order to meet the need to strengthen the democratic legitimacy of the newly created European Union, taking account of the fact that the effectiveness of the process of European integration required the Union to move closer to the citizen.

The presence of representatives of the regional and local levels in the institutional structure of the Community is the outcome of a long process characterised by two essential conditions. On the one hand the principle of institutional autonomy, which governs the implementation of Community law in the Member States, is based on the assumption that those Community rules that touch on issues that fall within the sphere of responsibility of the regional and/or local authorities of each Member State are applied by the latter in accordance with national legal arrangements. If these authorities help to prepare Community rules, they logically feel more responsible for guaranteeing the correct application thereof and this in turn enhances the effectiveness of the process of European integration. On the other hand, in order to shape the future of the European Union, the expectations of its citizens must be made known. This already occurs within the European Parliament, an institution elected via direct universal suffrage, as well as within the European Council and Council of the European Union, which represent the citizens as nationals of the Member States. The involvement of regional and local authorities opens up a new possibility for the participation of citizens at that level. Therefore, the Committee of the Regions was established in order to enable the Union to adapt to the new situation created by changes made to the organisational structures of the Member States, developments in Community regional policy, and by the decision to create the European Union.

Bringing the principles of effectiveness and democratic legitimacy together within the Committee of the Regions has not always been an easy task and has led to numerous debates. As indicated above, since the entry into force of the Nice Treaty, all members of the Committee have been required to hold electoral office or be directly accountable to an elected assembly. This condition reinforces the role of the Committee as a pillar of the democratic legitimacy of the European Union, but in some cases it can impede the smooth functioning of the Committee. The elected members, who also have responsibilities in their regional and local authorities, are not always available to attend the Committee's meetings and participate in its work. In order to apply the provisions of the Treaties effectively, this contradiction must be overcome by ensuring these two principles (effectiveness and democratic legitimacy) are complementary.

On the other hand, the democratic legitimacy of the members of the Committee enhances the legitimacy of the Committee itself, rendering it more effective in supporting its own position in the inter-institutional dialogue. As the Committee is a purely consultative body, it relies on this underpinning in order to be able to influence the process of European integration. Furthermore, the broad interpretation made possible by the wording used ("to hold an electoral mandate or be politically accountable to an elected assembly") and the equal numbers of alternates and members in the Committee have from the outset resolved any practical difficulties related to the democratic legitimacy of its members. The Congress of Local and Regional Authorities of the Council of Europe is another body that has an equal number of alternates and members. It is a feature that is well suited to such bodies, responsible for representing the interests of sub-national authorities within international organisations. The legal status of alternate members is not entirely clear. In some cases, the list of alternates is used by the Committee to access a larger number of regional or local bodies, while in other cases, above all when dealing with regional bodies that have their own legislative powers, both members and alternates are drawn from the same body. In all cases the aim is to make the organisation operate more efficiently. It is also important to note that, in terms of the requirement for democratic legitimacy, the Treaty does not distinguish between alternates and members.

In essence, by embodying both the principles of democratic legitimacy and effectiveness, the Committee of the Regions is one step closer to achieving its aims for the future. It has similar characteristics to those of the Council and European Parliament. As at the Council, its members fulfil a specific role within the government structure of their Member State. And, its internal workings and organisation resemble those of an assembly such as the European Parliament. The Committee can nonetheless be distinguished from these other bodies in that its members are divided into national delegations, political groups and inter-regional groups. However, as the body which represents the regional and local levels within the process of European integration, as outlined above, the Committee of the Regions is subject to certain limitations.

3. Representation of diversity in the process of European integration

The regional and local authorities of the Member States are diverse: their nature and powers vary, not only from one Member State to another, but also within Member States. The process of European integration therefore does not have an equal impact on all regional and local bodies in the Member States. Nonetheless, this diversity has not led to unequal treatment within the Committee of the Regions, which has adopted a uniform approach in this respect. Indeed this is its most significant distinguishing feature. However, this does cast some doubt on the Committee's legitimacy and effectiveness.

As a constituent part of an international organisation, the Committee is plenary by nature. It comprises representatives of all of the Member States, although some regional and local authorities are not directly represented. Moreover, the division of seats among the Member States does not take account of the number or characteristics of these authorities, nor of the number of people they represent. Rather, the Committee of the Regions uses the same distribution scheme as the Economic and Social Committee. Against this background, the Treaty stipulates that the members of the Committee of the Regions must act in a wholly independent manner in the general interest of the Community as a whole. It is difficult to combine the requirement for democratic legitimacy with this further condition of independence. How can an elected member or representative who is politically accountable to an elected assembly act independently of the interests of his region or municipality? This would seem to be a further contradiction. But only by adopting this role of general representation can a body such as the Committee of the Regions really matter within the process of European integration.

It would be impossible for all regional and local authorities of the Member States to be directly represented in a Community body. Those representatives appointed to the Committee bring with them a wealth of experience and personal knowledge, but the opinions issued by the Committee must reflect the interests of all regional and local bodies of the Member States. It is this joint interest for which the Committee of the Regions acts as a mouthpiece vis-à-vis the rest of the European Community. Its aim is to find ways of allowing diversity to be expressed and of promoting cooperation on the basis of a better awareness of the situations of others.

On several occasions in the past, the members of the Committee have been unable to reach a consensus and, consequently, have rejected an opinion proposed. However, it is important to note that this Community body is not, and must not be, the only forum through which the regional and local levels are able to participate in the process of European integration. Despite the diversity of its members, the Committee presents a united front, and this prevents it from fully meeting their individual needs. This can happen for example with respect to those regional authorities that have their own legislative powers. The presence of representatives of such bodies within the Committee goes some way towards explaining its desire to share in the co-decision process alongside the European Parliament and the Council. However, these bodies are also able to sit on the Council, as representatives of their Member State. In any event, in order to ensure that the participation of the regional and local levels in the process of integration is effective, over and above the seats they hold on the Committee of the Regions, further methods are needed to give them a more specific role. They must not be restricted to participating at Community level alone, rather a constant dialogue must be established between the different levels of government within each Member State. Only by taking account of the situation in each Member State can the challenges of diversity be effectively overcome.

All in all, in order to strengthen the role played by the Committee of the Regions in the process of European integration, its make-up must be reconsidered and better adapted to its specific form of legitimacy. The Treaty does not provide for the participation of regional and local bodies in the process of electing the members of the Committee; rather they are proposed by the Member States and appointed by a Council decision. Although in practice the national proposals are drawn up after consulting national associations of regional and local authorities, their role should be explicitly defined in order to guarantee that the Committee is truly representative. From this point of view, it is also worth questioning the logic behind leaving the final decision for the appointment of the members in the hands of the Council, in particular given that its role is limited to approving the national proposals and that this in turn seriously hampers the smooth operation of the Committee.

4.   Final remarks

The Committee's role in representing the local and regional levels in the process of European integration is determined by its nature and legitimacy. Its aspirations are viewed with mistrust, both by the Member States and by the European Parliament. Thus, within the framework of representation of interests and recognition of powers which characterises the entire institutional structure of the Community, the regional and local levels participate via a purely consultative body. Although for the time being there are no substantial differences between the legal status of the institutions and bodies of the Community, the role of the institutions enjoys greater political recognition, while the bodies are to a certain extent dependent on the institutions. The Committee of the Regions is rather poorly placed in the machinery of European integration.

However, in view of the nature of the entities it represents, the Committee has reasserted its status as a political body, approving an annual work programme based on its own political priorities. The Committee has not contented itself with the consultative role conferred upon it in the Treaty as part of the process of adopting Community laws, but also makes use of its power of initiative to make its voice heard in the major debates surrounding the process of European integration. In its desire to obtain greater recognition it has developed a considerable network of contacts both within and outside the institutional structures of the Community. Its dialogue with representatives of regional and local bodies in the applicant countries has been particularly significant. Enlargement – a major challenge for the European Union – will have a direct impact on the Committee of the Regions, given that the states concerned overwhelmingly have highly centralised systems of government. In this respect, the Committee has adopted a strategy based on emphasising the need to strengthen the local and regional levels of government in these states so as to enable them to take on their rightful roles as new Member States.

Essentially, despite the teething difficulties the Committee of the Regions has faced, which were only to be expected, the work it has done over its first ten years can be viewed in a positive light. In addition to achievements made in terms of its legal status (referred to above), the new Treaty includes in its objectives the territorial dimension of economic and social cohesion policy, requiring the Union to respect local and regional autonomy, albeit on the basis of the Constitutions of the Member States and subject to the explicit duty to uphold the essential tasks of the state, including in particular guaranteeing the territorial integrity of the state.

The role of the Committee of the Regions in the future of Europe will depend on exactly what that future brings. More than fifty years have passed since the preamble to the Treaty of Paris, signed in 1951, made reference to the "destiny henceforward shared" of the peoples of Europe. And yet the exact nature of that destiny has still not been defined. The systems in place today are still overwhelmingly intergovernmental. Indeed the obstacles faced during the negotiations for the Treaty establishing a Constitution for Europe are characteristic of this. Although the text is described as a Constitution, its nature and the majority of its provisions make it more like an international treaty. The aims of the Committee of the Regions fit in perfectly with the establishment of a new European political and organisational model. As part of that debate, the creation of a third pillar of democratic legitimacy anchored in the regional and local levels is easily justified. New forms of citizen participation are needed to take account of the diversity of the peoples of Europe and their everyday lives. But unless major changes are made to the very nature of the Union, moving away from the principles of inter-state relations, the participation of regional and local authorities will remain an issue of domestic law and, consequently, the goals of those authorities will have to be dealt with via the legal systems of each Member State.

Stefaan De Rynck, Institut universitaire européen, Florence

The politics of change: education and environment policy in the Communities and Regions of Belgium

Policy change, European governance and the Role of the Regions

Over recent decades, the Belgian institutional structure in which inter-regional similarities and differences evolve has altered radically. Institutional change has stressed mutual differences between the regions more than similarities, and granted substantial policy autonomy to sub-state government. Linguistic and cultural differences as well as a diverging economic fortune North and South of the linguistic border contributed to the federalisation of what was once a highly centralised state. The 1993 constitutional revision proclaimed Belgium officially as a federal state, as the end result of a process of various constitutional changes initiated in 1970.

Does Regional Government Matter for Public Policy?

This process has been studied from various angles, including nationalism, social movements, citizens' feelings of identity and allegiance with the central state and/or the regional entities, the constitutional arrangements as such and the elaborate mechanisms of checks-and-balances in national decision-making. The possible impact of regionalisation on public policy, however, has barely been analysed. The question of the possible impact of newly installed regional governments on policy choices requires an analysis of the links between political-institutional change and public policy change. Any such impact would then have to be analysed in terms of direction and intensity of policy change, with an in-depth explanation for any such change.

That regional government would automatically have an effect on public policy cannot be taken for granted for various reasons. Some authors observe alleged policy convergences between European states; how then could regions within a state diverge? Others point to global and domestic constraints on policy change, including the well-known path-dependence whereby regional policy would inevitably have to build upon the national policy legacy already in place before regionalisation. A strong demand for regional autonomy could certainly be disappointed by the inertia of an entrenched policy paradigm.

Looking into the question of the link between institutional and policy change requires a comparison between highly different policy sectors. This paper looks at education and agri-environmental policy since their regionalisation in 1988. It studies a period of ten years until the end of 1999. Studying agri-environmental policy allows for analysing the policy impact of regionalisation in a European context. Herein, Belgian regions are involved in policy-making within the context of established European legislation, with harmonised quality standards. This European context would predict some degree of uniformity amongst the policies in the regions, in spite of a differing socio-economic context. What was found in the case of Flanders, however, was a political process largely driven by regional politics, and much less by EU related elements. The policy outcome of this regional process was then cosmetically presented to the EU as being part of the requirements imposed by European legislation.

Education policy was chosen as a second case because of the highly similar socio-economic context in both regions[1], at least for the particular case of education policy as demonstrated by De Rynck (2002)[2]. Yet, it is also here that the greatest policy variation between the Flemish and French Community appears, with radical changes in Flanders since the end of the 1980s and incremental changes only in the French Community, in spite of higher "pressure for policy change" in the latter case.

The Difficulties of Changing Public Policy – Explaining Policy Change

When has a public policy really changed? Policy change should be defined by looking at both the intensity and direction of change. Herein, a typology of public policy based on who pays and who benefits is a useful tool. Cost-bearers and beneficiaries can be well-organised in pressure groups, or they can be present as atomised individuals in society, leading to four different patterns of politics.

---

[1]   The term "region" is used in a generic sense, here to refer to the Flemish and French Communities.
[2]   De Rynck (Stefaan), *Changing Public Policy: The Role of the Regions,* Brussels, PIE Lang, 2002.

Figure: **Policy Typology According to Wilson**[3]

	Benefits	
	Diffuse	Concentrated
Diffuse	Majoritarian Politics	Client Politics

	Costs	
Concentrated	Entrepreneurial Politics	Interest-Group Politics

Wilson's client politics corresponds to Lowi's distributive policy[4]. Entrepreneurial politics corresponds to regulatory policy, and interest-group politics to redistribution. A distributive policy is characterised by the ease with which a policy can be disaggregated and dispensed, unit by small unit. Highly individualised decisions pay little attention to the common good. In many instances, "the most influential among [the deprived] can be accommodated by further disaggregation of the stakes". In short, distributive policies are characterised by "pork barrel politics". Regulatory policies involve "a direct choice as to who will be indulged and who deprived". Rules are stated in general terms, and their implementation occurs on a case-by-case basis in an impartial manner. The impact of regulation raises costs for some and expands the "alternatives of private individuals". In redistributive policies, the categories of impact are much broader and approach social classes. Issues that involve redistribution are heavily contentious, as for instance shown by the European Union's financial perspectives.

Public policies have a tendency to evolve into a so-called distributive logic, with well-organised beneficiaries and a diffuse cost structure. That kind of logic tends to become entrenched. It is well documented that any political system and policy sector encounters considerable difficulties when attempting to change such a policy. Three forms of political behaviour are oriented towards the status-quo rather than change. These are "blame avoidance" strategies by political actors, who are averse to running the risk of upsetting organised beneficiaries of existing policy; the exchange of

---

[3]   Wilson (James Q.), *Political Organizations*, New York, Basic Books, 1973, 330-337.

[4]   Lowi (Theodore J.), *American Business, Public Policy, Case Studies and Political Theory, World Politics*, 16(1964), 667-715. Following quotes are from pages 690-691.

political authority for selective (often electoral) benefits, leading to an accommodating policy style; the co-opting of new and protesting policy participants in the mainstream policy process. Furthermore, a "consociational democracy" such as Belgium encounters specific difficulties for changing a policy.

Nevertheless, there are also several factors that offer structural opportunities for change, such as external shocks and strain; party political adaptation, often linked to elections; and a number of events linked to routine politics, such as the yearly budgetary process. Clearly, there is a tension between policy stability and the dynamics of change. Plural democracies will promote political and social entrepreneurs whose actions will aim at a redistribution of policy costs and benefits. Their behaviour will be the opposite of office-holders who "seek above all not to maximize the credit they receive but to minimize blame [and be ...] good policy satisficers"[5]. Policy entrepreneurs are political and social actors who invest their time, resources and reputation in advancing policy change. In other words, entrepreneurs are the opposite of policy brokers, who are "more concerned with system stability than with achieving policy goals"[6]. While entrepreneurship is linked to change and the generation of policy conflict in the search for new goals, brokerage focuses on stability and appeasement.

In spite of its importance, the phenomenon of entrepreneurship is not well studied in public policy. More knowledge exists on how individuals arrive at important political and administrative positions than about their impact on the policy debate. "The arrow from recruitment and background to leadership behaviour and skills is remarkably indeterminate"[7], perhaps because the concatenation of particular leaders with particular historical contexts is a matter of chance rather than necessity, leading to a low probability of social and political change. Furthermore, policy incrementalism, structural approaches to interest intermediation, and political culture approaches all stress the continuity of the policy process, regardless of the movements of personnel. Institutional analysis often emphasises the constraints that decision-makers face rather than the opportunities they create. Rational choice focuses on actors' adaptation to expectation and situation, rather than on how actors shape expectation and situation.

---

[5]   Weaver (Kent), "The Politics of Blame Avoidance", *Journal of Public Policy*, 6(1986), 372.

[6]   Sabatier (Paul A.), "Towards Better Theories of the Policy Process", *Political Science and Politics*, June 1991, 153.

[7]   Aberbach (Joel D.) & Rockman (Bert A.), "Does Governance Matter - And If So, How? Process, Performance and Outcomes", Governance, 5(1992), 145.

At the time of regionalisation of education policy at the end of the 1980s, the national policy in place had evolved into a highly distributive type of policy. Although faced with a similar situational context, the Flemish and French Communities have chosen a radically different course since regionalisation in 1988. In Flanders, changes in the planning system testify to a new view of the role of the state as well as the local schools. The central state has placed itself in the role of an enabler, rather than being a party directly involved in delivering education. This has also had radical consequences on the system of quality control of all schools, be they local, Catholic or state schools.

In contrast, the French Community consolidated the national policy legacy, and attempts at moving away from that legacy have failed. De Rynck (2002) explains these changes in greater detail, by analysing education delivery, public funding and the input and management of human resources. The work also analyses in-depth the political discussion on the conditions, if any, public policies should impose on education providers that receive public funding, and at which level decision-making for various issues should lie. As a conclusion, it is shown that Flemish education policy has evolved from a distributive type of policy into a regulatory type. Providers of education currently face a structurally different situation compared to the national regime in place before regionalisation. No such changes happened in the French Community.

To understand the variation in the patterns of policy change, the difference in Socialist Party adaptation in both Communities is crucial. Policy entrepreneurs in Flanders in that party had more space to take risks and pursue reform compared to their French speaking colleagues, who were constrained in the 1990s by the risk of a strong party fragmentation related to proposed policy innovations. This can be explained in relation to party features, wider social forces and interest representation. Also, policy in Flanders never changed radically at any juncture in time. Rather, it altered gradually over the course of a decade, by building upon previous decisions.

The discussion on "quality" of education was heavily affected by the role of the publicly funded Catholic schools and the amount of permissible state control on their activities in both Communities. The outcome of this discussion is somewhat counter-intuitive. While the Catholic Church in Flanders is much stronger politically and socially, its constitutionally guaranteed "freedom to organise education" has been more constrained compared to the situation in the French Community since 1988. Again, policy entrepreneurship seizing upon structural opportunities for change is important to understand such an outcome.

Intensive Livestock Production: Profits versus Pollution in Flanders and Wallonia since 1988

A second case concerns policy change in the agri-environmental sector, particularly with regard to intensive livestock production. The starting point in time (1988) is consistent with the analysis of education policy. The Flemish case is theoretically the most interesting one for understanding the phenomenon of policy change. Compared to the case of education policy, the social pressure to change policy was much higher in the agri-environmental case in Flanders. It was also much higher compared to agri-environmental policy in Wallonia. Pressure for radical change was moreover supported by the European Union. Yet, actual change was much more incremental and hesitant compared to the case of education policy, in particular due to the high risk of party dissent within the Christian-Democratic Party, which was constantly in power during the reference period (1988-1999). Party and party system features, which have limited the discretion of policy entrepreneurs within the Socialist Party but especially also within the Christian-Democratic Party itself, explain this to a large extent. These features themselves are linked to the representation of farmers and environmental groups in the policy process, which also display significant differences between the two regions. As a result, agri-environmental policy has remained a distributive type of policy in Flanders, in spite of the introduction of some features which are more characteristic of a regulatory policy.

The Politics of Policy Change Compared

To sum up, the most radical policy change was found in Flemish education policy, whereas Flemish agri-environmental policy and the French Community education policy were subject to much higher societal and EU pressure for change. It is to an explanation of this paradox that this paper now turns.

Clearly, the capacity and desire of newly established regional governments to formulate and implement policy change do not only vary across regions, but also across policy sectors within a region. In particular, policy change is affected by the coincidence of opportunities for reform and the presence of policy entrepreneurs. Such coincidence emerges in a region-specific manner, but also varies across policy sectors, as shown by the case studies.

Indeed, in terms of the impact of regionalisation on policy change, there is a strong variation between policy sectors in a single region, namely between education and environment policy in Flanders. Although it would be tempting to attribute such variation to sector-specific features (in line with public policy theories such as advocacy coalitions or policy networks), De Rynck (2002) manages to go beyond this argument and trace the fundamental driving forces behind various policy developments back to factors related to regional politics.[8] Policy arenas are embedded in a specific territorial context, with elections and political party systems that mediate between society and state powers. The link between functionally divided policy systems and eventual authoritative decisions runs through the same political mechanism and party system, which reflects the dominant social and political cleavages of the past and present society[9].

More specifically, political parties have played a crucial role in all cases, and the action and discretion of policy actors were strongly affected by regional politics and power structures, which imposed a common logic on all sectors. In the end, the findings on policy change at sectoral level in both regions are related to party adaptation or its absence. The drive for change in Flemish education policy, at least for the radical restructuring in the delivery of the service with renewed quality control, and in agri-environmental policy was situated in the renewal of the Flemish Socialist Party. The success in Flemish education policy change was due to the receptive Christian-Democratic Party, which was only natural given the fact that Socialists started renouncing their traditional role of protecting public schools. The failure in agri-environmental policy was related to the inability of the Christian-Democrats in Flanders to respond to the environmental voice in their party and elsewhere, and redefine their organisational and electoral relationship with the farm lobby. Entrepreneurship within the party at times when they controlled the environment portfolio was suppressed. This development was largely affected by the risk of

---

[8] Neither could it be argued that the observed diversity should be traced back to variation in the functional imperatives of the policy, be they economic, social or geographic imperatives.

[9] Even strong forces that disperse decision-making authority into more functionally organised multi-level systems have not broken that link, as was shown in the Europeanised case of agri-environmental policy, where domestic Flemish structures prevailed over European obligations.

increasing internal party fragmentation that would follow from a redefinition of the relationship of the party with the farm organisations. Risk of party fragmentation in the Socialist party with regards to its renewed position on education policy was also present, but strongly marginalised due to the impact of party leadership and the weaker position of support groups in society. In the Southern part of the country, the absence of renewal from the side of the Parti Socialiste towards the environmental issue explains the inertia in agri-environmental policy to a large extent. Non-party adaptation also accounts for the stalemate in the education field in spite of a high pressure for change.

At a more general level, this paper also shows that the innovative impact of newly created regional governments on public policy depends on more than the simple establishment of new political institutions. New regional institutions do not generate policy change as such. They redefine the context for actors' calculations and behaviour, and have a complex influence on governmental capabilities. Moreover, regionalisation might be a strategic move by powerful political actors to maintain or restore an old political order which they risk losing in the national context. Too often, political scientists seem to take for granted that new institutions are an element of political innovation, while political actors might interpret regions as a tool for sustaining the power and position of centrality in policy-making, which they risk losing at national level. The question to what extent a newly established regional institution can account for maintaining the national policy legacy is certainly understudied.

By tracing dynamics, this research has demonstrated how politics affects policy change more than institutions or policy pressure. Political action engaged in restructuring the legacy of the past, sometimes through the unintended consequences of policy decisions, sometimes in deliberate attempts to alter the distribution of power. This movement was stronger in Flanders, perhaps because of its stronger demand for regional autonomy in the first place. Also important was the desire of the dominant Socialist actor in the French Community to maintain or consolidate the national legacy in education. By holding the political-institutional context largely constant (i.e. by looking at different policy in highly similar regional political systems within one country), this research has demonstrated that politics engaged differently in making sense of the new regions.

Such dynamic analysis and process-tracing avoids the chicken and egg problem that contrived static pictures impose on institutions and political action. Some would argue to the contrary of these findings and contend that current political office-holders in the two Communities reason and act differently because of an ultimate divergence in political culture, or because of differences in informal rules of the game. De Rynck (2002) makes a convincing case against such static pairing of factors by deducing the policy of the year 2000 from party adaptation, political action and strategies of the 1990s and before. These elements can of course gradually introduce and reinforce cultural differences between the regions.

Consequences for European Integration

The above findings lead to some considerations on regions in European Union governance. Modes of European governance are likely to change considerably over the next decade. Internationalisation, changing technology, shifts in patterns of political loyalty and identity are redefining established political institutions and their boundaries. Already, many functions traditionally exercised by the European nation-state have been moved upwards to the European Union level and downwards to regional or other sub-state governments. This development has often been presented as the "twin challenge" to the nation-state.

In the future European governance, it is indeed highly likely that regional actors, and certainly those with legislative powers, will play an enhanced role for various reasons. Certainly, increased incidence of regionalisation has appeared in many countries over the most recent decades and years. Devolution referenda for Scotland and Wales were one of the first campaign promises the Blair government put into action. The Italian Parliament currently discusses a transfer of a considerable block of responsibilities from the national to the regional level, including education which has played an important role in the unification of the country. This Italian reform builds on the regionalisation as decided under the previous centre-left government. The French Constitution as adjusted in 2003 enshrines regional government for the first time, and allows for regional policy experiments. The formerly unitary countries of Belgium and Spain were of course regionalised already a few decades ago.

It might be tempting to conclude from these various observations that a process of institutional convergence has started in the European Union. In this process, Europe would be assumed to provide a general and unifying policy framework to the increased breakdown of and fragmentation within the traditional nation-state. In the same spirit of convergence, it is taken for granted that regions and the European Union level are natural allies in a process of building new institutions.

Yet, the findings of this research shed doubts on this view. It is well documented that the integration of policies in the European Union has been driven by a highly fragmented system of sectoral networks. A first sight, the result of this study on the impact of newly established regional governments in Belgium on public policy seems to confirm that a "post-national" Europe is being constructed along functional lines. Indeed, policy variation since regionalisation is not only found across regions in the Belgian case, but also across policy sectors *within* regions. However, this phenomenon results less from policy sector-specific features and sectoral fragmentation than from overall power structures in Belgian regional politics, as explained above, and its redefinition at a new level of territory.

This emphasis on the importance of territory as a coherent whole and a political entity appears as being at odds with the functional organisation and policy fragmentation of the European Union. Overcoming this contradiction and recognising regions as unified political systems based on profound social and political changes, rather than as collections of sectoral policy networks, will be crucial for the future European governance system. Already, the first signs of disaffection from the EU by stronger regions in Germany and elsewhere have emerged in the post-Nice debate on the future of the Union.

Two further lessons on the future role of regions in the EU should be drawn from this study. First, it cannot be taken for granted that region-building responds to a similar logic in the various European countries and even within countries, as sometimes assumed by European Institutions. The construction of new political spaces at regional level in various countries is a complex process that involves common factors, but it is also affected by the specific social and institutional contexts wherein which region-building occurs, and mediated by the incidence of political leadership. Such leadership is particularly crucial at the time of establishing new regional institutions. Given the strong variation that can be detected within one small Member State such as Belgium, any sweeping generalisation on the future role of regions in the European Union should be treated with caution.

Second, in the future European governance, the European Union is likely to be confronted with a wider diversity of policy outcomes due to the process of regionalisation and the continued (renewed?) importance of territory. This process will come on top of enlargement, which will already lead to a larger number of policy preferences in the political system of the EU than is currently the case. In this paper, it was demonstrated that this statement even holds in the case of EU policy, or at least in one case of agri-environmental policy, where a similar EU directive was treated very differently by different regions in one country. It is questionable whether the draft Constitution for the European Union gives sufficient answers to cope with the increased number of policy actors and preferences, in spite of its progress in terms of recognising the regional dimension in the process of European integration.

2001/2002

TRANS-EUROPEAN COOPERATION: HOW CAN REGIONS AND CITIES HELP TO CREATE A CONTINENT WITHOUT BORDERS?

Chairman of the jury

Mr Johannes Flensted-Jensen, President of Århus County Council, Denmark.

Theses submitted

NUMBER OF ENTRANTS	LANGUAGES		COUNTRY	
16	5	German English Spanish French Italian	7	Germany Austria Spain France Ireland Italy United Kingdom

Winners:

First prize:

Mr Olivier Castric (FR), *What kind of partnerships for the regions of the European Union?*, University of Rennes I

Second prize:

Mr Matthew Cannon (IE), *The Channel Tunnel Case Study: Policy Networks and the Emergence of a European Meso – The Transmanche Euroregion*, University of Limerick

Olivier Castric, University of Rennes I

What kind of partnerships for the regions of the European Union?

At the beginning of this new century, the European Union (EU) is preparing for a significant enlargement. The EU will eventually have around 500 million citizens. Creating a continent without borders on this scale constitutes a major challenge. If the Union is to continue to function in this context, it is important, according to the Commission, to develop new kinds of partnership between the different levels of government in Europe. Partnership implies two or more partners coming together to form a closer relationship to achieve a common goal. It often involves political, economic, social, and other forms of dialogue before it is transcribed into a legal framework. The treaties define neither partnership nor the partners, but the process of EU integration involves a considerable number of them, many of which are transnational in nature: the partnership between the Community and the regions, among the regions themselves, transnational partnerships of businesses, economic and social partners, and the partnership between the Union, the Member States and third countries, among others. Applied to the regions, it becomes a principle in the rules governing the Structural Funds (1). The concept is also present in the form of cooperation between regions of different Member States (2). Elected by universal suffrage, local and regional authorities are an integral part of the system of government within the European Union. In this respect, they have a role to play in the good governance of the Union and in the creation of a continent without borders. The partnership principle has a contribution to make here(3).

1.   Vertical partnership for the implementation of the Union's policies

Introduced in 1988[1] as part of the regulatory framework governing the implementation of the Structural Funds, the partnership is now defined by Article 8 of Regulation 1260/99: "close consultation between the Commission and the Member State, together

---

[1]   Council Regulation (EEC) No 2052/88 of 24 June 1988 on the tasks of the Structural Funds and their effectiveness and on coordination of their activities between themselves and with the operations of the European Investment Bank and the other existing financial instruments, OJ L 185, 15.7.1988, p. 9, amended by Council Regulation (EEC) No. 2081/93 of 20 July 1993, OJ L 193, 31.7.1993, p. 5.

with the authorities and bodies designated by the Member State within the framework of its national rules and current practices, namely: the regional and local authorities and other competent public authorities, the economic and social partners, [and] any other relevant competent bodies within this framework."[2]. The principle, which is based on the subsidiarity principle, has acquired a specificity whose autonomy is nonetheless open to discussion. The declaration on the future of the European Union adopted by the Laeken Council on 14 and 15 December 2001 mentions, for the first time at this level, the place of the regions in the debate on the division and definition of competencies within the European Union[3]. The spirit of subsidiarity does not date from the TEU. The Commission has stated that the concept of partnership already reflected this concern[4]. The introduction of subsidiarity into the Treaty was broadly considered to be a step forward in that the principle is an expression of the desire for improved arrangements for exercising powers. However, it is difficult to ensure that it is applied identically in all the Member States, each of which has a different concept of it.

Subsidiarity, which is more of a behavioural obligation than a legal one[5], would probably be strengthened further by the systematic application of the partnership between the Community, the Member States, and the regions. This could help to avoid "border disputes" between exclusive and shared competencies. It should be possible for everything the Community does to be carried out on the basis of the partnership between the Community, the Member States, and the regions, according to the competencies of each. When the Community acts and, as is often the case, this action has an effect on the regions, it would make it easier for it to know the extent to which it should act and to measure the effects of its action if those on the receiving end of those effects help to define that action. Partnership needs to go beyond consultation. It should enable the Community, where appropriate, to moderate and adjust its action in the public interest and in the interest of democracy. In this respect, a certain amount of ambiguity between proximity and subsidiarity becomes apparent. All the Union's decisions must respect proximity. Whilst proximity, like cohesion, is an objective and not a principle, any action aimed at achieving this objective must comply with the

---

[2]   Council Regulation (EC) No. 1260/1999 of 21 June 1999 laying down general provisions on the Structural Funds, OJ L 161, 26.6.1999 p.1.
[3]   Conclusions of the Presidency, SN 300/01.
[4]   Commission Report on the workings of the TEU, 10/05/95, SEC (95) 731 final, paragraph 71.
[5]   Point 79 of the Presidency's conclusions from the Vienna European Council of December 1998.

principle of subsidiarity. As the EESC has indicated[6], the concepts of decision-making levels and of closeness to the citizen might lead one to suppose, wrongly, that subsidiarity is based solely on vertical, i.e. hierarchical and territorial, criteria. However, this proximity is not determined exclusively by territorial criteria; these are complemented by functional criteria. Enabling decisions to be taken as close as possible to citizens implies geographical and territorial closeness, but also, above all, participatory and representative closeness. The Committee of the Regions states that closeness is the source of democratic legitimacy[7]. However, this is better achieved by the free and democratic election of representatives. Participatory democracy, on which the partnership is based, relates to a collective subject that considers itself as such. But can one speak of a collective identity at European level, when this identity at national level is the people, and there is no such thing as a European people, but rather peoples of Europe? The peoples of the Member States are represented by the European Parliament[8]. Citizens are also represented by local and regional authorities, which are in turn represented at Community level by the Committee of the Regions. This representative system is linked, as required by proximity, with subsidiarity from Community level down to the regions. This is characterised by a participatory system that brings the regions and the Community together in partnership. The fact that the regions are represented in the Committee of the Regions also ensures that they have a role in the institutional partnership. In order to work properly, such a system needs to guarantee wide-ranging access to information on the activities of the partners and, at all levels, honest cooperation, which the Court has described as the corollary of partnership[9]. This does not mean, however, that it follows on from it as a matter of course.

2. Horizontal partnership for cooperation between regions

Twinning, transnational, cross-border, inter-regional and decentralised cooperation are all forms of partnership between cities and regions of different countries. The

---

[6]   Opinion 535/2001, op.cit., on Organised civil society and European governance: the Committee's contribution to the White Paper, point 3.6.

[7]   Report on proximity, 05/11/01, CdR 436/2001 fin, p. 6.

[8]   CJEC 29/10/80, Roquette v. Council, 138/79, ECR p. 3333, point 33. CJEC 29/10/80, Maïzena v. Council, 139/79, ECR p. 3393, point 34.
    See also CJEC 30/03/95, Parliament v. Council, C-65/93, ECR p. I-643, point 21. CJEC 05/07/95, Parliament v. Council, C-21/94, ECR p. I-1827, point 17. CJEC 10/06/97, Parliament v. Council, C-392/95, ECR p. I-3213, point 14.

[9]   CJEC 05/10/99, Netherlands v Commission, C-84/96, point 47.

existence of the process of European integration is not indispensable to the emergence and development of such cooperation. It cannot be denied, however, that it has played, and continues to play, a key role in the rise and spread of these partnerships. Since these two processes share the same fundamentals, notably the desire to maintain peace, they have converged and become interdependent. The Single European Act, which defines the Internal Market as an area without internal frontiers, has brought the Member States and their devolved authorities into direct competition within the Community within a context of the internationalisation of trade. By allowing the free movement of people, goods, services and capital, European integration has reduced the physical effects of borders and helped to change the way people perceive them. At the same time, by putting Europe's economies in competition with one another in a way that has often been painful in highly competitive sectors of activity, it has made cooperation, not only between states but also between sub-state authorities, more and more necessary. The Community's attitude towards cooperation between cities and regions has progressively moved in the direction of positive encouragement by the EU to develop such horizontal partnerships, sometimes including cities and regions of third countries. The Community acts to encourage and initiate those partnerships that cannot adequately be put in place by Member States due to their lack of appropriate legal frameworks and of a level of subsidiarity that involves the regional actors that are closest to the citizens in certain policies and actions, whose optimum effectiveness is thus ensured. The principles for action must be consistent, as the common goal is to help strengthen cohesion. The future challenge of cooperation between cities and regions lies in strengthening the partnership between regional and local authorities, and the economic and social partners who are in touch with the practicalities of the trend on the other. This is one of the basic principles of regional policy and a driving force behind regional economic development. The benefits of enshrining cooperation between cities and regions as a matter of Community policy are largely to be found in the specifics of that cooperation. It makes it possible, through working together, to look at ideas, methods and practices. Everyone involved can thus question their working practices and draw lessons from those of their partners in order to make improvements. The aim is not to transpose successful experiences at any cost, as this does not always work. Rather, the aim is to improve the partners' access, whatever their level, to policies that, by virtue of their horizontal aspect and their territorial impact, are considered essential to the reduction of regional disparities. Cooperation between cities and regions, by virtue of the partnerships it creates and implies between actors, makes it possible to overcome the concerns about inter-regional cooperation in terms of competition between regions and to reach a level of cooperation that looks for complementarity. Thus, the idea is to strengthen cohesion by involving actors from deprived regions in cooperation networks. In line with the subsidiarity principle, it is not the Community's job to replace players from Member States. However, it does have a role to play by acting as a catalyst for change and as a broker of best practice. In this way, it also satisfies the requirement that the Union be close to its citizens.

3. The partnership principle: a principle for the good governance of the Union

Governance can be defined as the "capacity of human societies to establish systems of representation, of institutions, of processes, of social bodies, to manage themselves in a voluntary movement"[10]. Governing the Union well means that governance, which is linked to the principles of subsidiarity and proximity, strengthens the effectiveness of European policies through the increased decentralisation, democracy, transparency and participation that partnership makes possible. European governance is not simply a matter of the relationship between the Union and governmental and non-governmental players. It applies right across the network of relationships between spheres of government within and between Member States. Local and regional authorities, which are elected by universal suffrage, are part of that. The EU must make its workings easier to understand, more transparent and more efficient by means of active subsidiarity with wide use of partnerships. The Committee of the Regions has stated that an interpretation of subsidiarity based solely on the matter of vertical division of power between different levels of government is too narrow[11]. The Committee calls for a "partnership of equality" and an "open coordination procedure" between the different "spheres of government". The aim of such an approach would be to seek the terms of a collective agreement on the conditions for success of public action, and thus to achieve a policy process characterised both by the wide range of perspectives apparent in modern society and by ongoing opportunities for each of those perspectives to be enriched through interaction with the others[12]. Some states are not yet very familiar with these mechanisms. In the French democratic tradition, it

---

[10]   Calame, P. and Talmant, A., *L'Etat au cœur, le Meccano de la gouvernance*, Desclée de Brouwer, Paris, 1997, p. 19.

[11]   CoR opinion 182/2000 of 14 December 2000 on *New Forms of Governance: Europe, a framework for citizens' initiative*, point II.2.

[12]   Lebessis, N. and Paterson, J., *Developing new modes of governance*, European Commission, Forward Studies Unit Working Paper, June 2000, p. 36.

is the duty of the centralised state to represent the public interest, and universal suffrage is the sole basis for democratic legitimacy. The European Union brings into play other means of legitimisation and democratic control: sharing of sovereignty freely agreed to between the constituent nations, monitoring of the constitutionality of laws by judicial bodies, thus demonstrating the independence, indeed the supremacy, of European judicial power. This does nothing to contradict the perception that it currently suffers from a democratic deficit. The accusations that continue to be made concerning the Union's democratic deficit hold back attempts at reform, to the extent that the options being considered remain wedded to the model of representative democracy. However, it could be said that the increasing decentralisation of Community action, bearing the hallmarks of subsidiarity, proximity and partnership, will convince nation states of its benefits in terms of effectiveness of the action. Given this concern that democracy be respected, it is up to nation states to involve all their levels of authority in the European dynamic. Making partnership with the local authorities that are closest to the citizen the general rule may appear to be a guarantee of democracy, but it does raise the issue of its efficiency in certain countries. To what extent do the Member States' administrative institutions lend themselves to these kinds of partnership? To what extent are they capable of obtaining the greatest possible advantage from the Community dynamic and of correcting any local imbalances that this dynamic may bring about within their country[13]? The renewed impetus with which devolution is currently taking shape, especially in France, and the spread of partnership will undoubtedly need to go hand in hand with a stronger presence of the State, possibly by means of more effective devolution in order to contain the rise of these local authorities, some of whom may be attracted by the idea of a Europe of Regions. Codifying partnership militates against such a system. Just as the scenario of a Europe of Regions that denies the fundamental role of nation states must be rejected, so must the fundamentally anti-integrationist vision of a "pick and mix" Europe that would give nation states complete freedom to carry out only those policies that suited them[14]. Codifying partnership must also go hand in hand with strengthening the strategic role of the Union. European integration and devolution both fulfil the need, recognised by the State itself, to entrust certain public service functions to authorities other than itself. However, they do not merely involve a technical rearrangement of the sharing of powers among public authorities. They have

---

[13]   Deloire, P., *La France, Maastricht et l'Europe des régions, regards sur l'actualité*, La documentation française No. 197, January 1994.

[14]   Raux, J, *Coopérations renforcées: une fausse bonne idée!* Ouest-France, 20.6.2000.

significant consequences for the nature of public action and the role of the State, which must adapt to them. At the present stage of European integration, the existence of sufficiently "competent" states that are capable, among other things, of creating places with collective identity and spaces for public debate, would appear to be the best guarantee against the risk of Europe disintegrating into a large number of regional or ethnic communities. Such a scenario would require a strong central authority at European level, which does not currently exist. The process itself of decision-making within the EU still gives rise to a subtle alchemy between political will, bureaucratic logic, and lobbying. By promoting the search for consensus and compromise, it can little by little influence national administrative practices, which, in many countries, are still characterised by a culture of conflict and arbitration. This culture may well enable decisions to be taken more quickly, but it is dangerous, because it brings a number of problems to a head and because it does not create optimal conditions for effective implementation of the decisions that have been taken closest to the citizen. As for the sense of belonging to the Union, this will certainly depend on its inhabitants being given more opportunities to experience European integration. A number of sectors are in need of real European strategies, or strengthening of existing ones: town and country planning, in particular the creation of networks of towns to coordinate urban policy; combating imbalances within Europe; trans-European networks to avoid the ills caused by excessive urbanisation; tourism and culture, to develop the European identity; and agriculture, in the face of global competition. This list, which is by no means exhaustive, shows the scale of the task to be achieved for and by the political Union, which will require the involvement of every level of government. In order to bring the EU and its citizens closer together, it is not sufficient to reduce the distance between them. It is also necessary to consider the nature of the relationship between the EU and its citizens. "It can no longer be a paternalistic relationship, but rather must be one of *partnership*."[15] To deal with the increase in the number of its members, the European Union must find ways to make its decision-making processes more efficient, to think up new ways of representation, and to strengthen the European executive. It will not be enough, however, for it to develop the traditional forms of democratic institutions. It must invent new ways of bringing citizens closer and involving them and their various forms of representation, including the regions, whilst drawing on information, communication, interactive discussion, and partnership. The principle of partnership could be included in the EU Constitution, which must lay down guiding and regulatory principles for the relations between the EU, the Member

---

[15]   Lebessis, N. and Paterson, J., *Developing new modes of governance*, op. cit., p. 15.

States, and sub-state authorities, thus enabling the EU to be as close as possible to its citizens. This would also mean involving citizens as partners in the fundamentalisation of the EU[16].

---

[16]   Blanchard, D. *La constitutionnalisation de l'Union européenne*, Apogée, Rennes, 2001, 476 p.

Matthew Cannon, Centre for European Studies - University of Limerick

The Channel Tunnel Case Study: Policy Networks and the Emergence of a European Meso – The Transmanche Euroregion

Abstract

The construction of the Channel Tunnel provides an opportunity to study co-operation at a number of levels in government. The central governments of the United Kingdom, France, and Belgium were crucial to the early stages of the Channel Tunnel. However, the inability of the central government to provide completely for the perceived impacts of a fixed link increased networking between subnational and supranational actors. The most notable innovation could be found at the subnational level, where trans-frontier co-operation emerged between localities in order to anticipate the expected impacts evolved into formal institutionalised arrangements. One of the first of these came in the formation of the *Transmanche* region which was developed specifically to deal with the immediate and expected impact of the Channel Tunnel and associated infrastructure. This consisted of formal contact between Kent County Council (KCC) and the Conseil Regional de Nord Pas de Calais (CRNPC). The advantages made evident through this form of co-operation led to an expansion of the region to include Flanders, Wallonia, and Brussels capital, thereby changing the *Transmanche* region into the *Transmanche Euroregion*. Ultimately this cross-border contact also led to a phenomenon known as third-level lobbying and the growth of networks between local as well as European officials. The extent to which these networks undercut the nation-state and create new trans-boundary loyalties and identities is a central part of the investigation in this thesis.

The purpose of this thesis is to examine a specific European meso-level subnational actor, in this case the trans-frontier grouping which has developed in the cross-channel area. The thesis examines transnational actors in the form of transfrontier co-operation between localities as well as subnational/supranational contact between European Union officials and cross-national regional bodies. The thesis uses the Channel Tunnel as a lens for understanding policy-making, while also examining the catalysing impact of the tunnel on the regions of Kent, Calais, Wallonia, Flanders and Brussels Capital.

Introduction

The development of the European Union has witnessed the interaction of regions more effectively across borders as national boundaries become increasingly open to spatial interrelationships[1]. Organised specific issues of common interest, transboundary regionalisation projects, reflect the opportunities and limitations presented by the institutional frameworks within which they operate[2]. Regionalism can undertake a variety of forms, and the economic regionalism of the Transmanche Euroregion is just one of many approaches[3]. The Transmanche Euroregion has emerged out of regional collaboration over economic, infrastructure and resource dependency resulting in an institutional structure that incorporates "transboundary regionalism" in a complex configuration that merges several tiers of governance[4].

Euroregions are mechanisms that enhance the exchange of information, organisational and economic resources of the regions; to help economic and social development of less advantaged areas[5]. Brunt (1995) refers to the Euroregion as a new geographical relationship, in which individually unique regions with certain similarities form a regional partnership. Thus, although the members of the grouping may differ in detail, they maintain many areas that may allow for co-operation, such as common problems of congestion, environmental degradation, and difficulties of urban renewal[6]. Trans-frontier groupings have become important actors in the socio-economic development process at the regional level; and they have exercised

---

[1]   Cappellin and Batey (1993).

[2]   Scott (1999b).

[3]   There are several types of regionalism, understood as politics aiming at making the regional entity a political subject, either to replace (separatism) or to supplement other levels of policy-making. Some regional political movements are associated with ethnic revivals within or across the nation states, others are based on functional aspects, acknowledging common problems and need for extended co-operation. A third variant might be rediscoveries of historical patterns of coexistence, communication and transactions across borders that up till recently where closed (Sem Fure, 1997).

[4]   Transboundary regionalism can be defined as a spatially integrated form of political co-operation and problem-solving that transcends the limits of nationally-based administrative practice and attempts to create (or re-create, as the case might be) a sense of cohesiveness, interdependence and common interests across national boundaries (Scott, 1999a).

[5]   Alomar (1995: 139).

[6]   Brunt (1995).

fundamental powers with regard to the delivery of social services over the regional territory through the inter-mediation of sub-regional governmental bodies. All of these activities are not attributes of only atypical or temporary actions of the more advanced and experimentally oriented regional bodies. They have become the defining elements of a new model of subnational government activity[7]. The Transmanche Euroregion provides a unique opportunity to examine the emergence of an efficacious and high profile Euroregion.

The Transmanche Euroregion has played a significant role in the development of Euroregions. Through the regions geographic position and high profile association with the Channel Tunnel, the Transmanche Euroregion has acted as a model for the development of additional Euroregions. The region consists of local and regional representatives from Kent, Nord Pas de Calais, Flanders, Wallonia and Brussels Capital, and was formed in 1991 by an international agreement between the subnational authorities agreeing to cross-border co-operation with the objective of limiting the negative effects of infrastructure and the Single European Market. The high profile nature of the Transmanche Euroregion is due in large part to the notoriety of its constituent regions. The inclusion of the Brussels, the 'capital' of Europe in the Transmanche Euroregion has added to the high profile nature of the region. Placing Brussels within a Euroregion has had important symbolic significance for the development of Euroregions on the whole. In addition the Transmanche Euroregion was one of the first regions to include a locality in the United Kingdom. With the initial success of the involvement of Kent in the European arena, other United Kingdom regions became interested in cross-border contact with other regions as well as developing cross-Channel networks.[8] The inclusion of Belgian regions has also drawn attention to the trans-frontier grouping as Wallonia and Flanders have both made efforts to support regional autonomy in the European Union. Flanders in particular has been prominent in the debate over regional autonomy, with its leader making the desire of the region for increased autonomy well known. The support for regional input is not solely left to the individual localities. Finally the connection between the Transmanche Euroregion, the Channel Tunnel and the construction of a Northern TGV system highlights the significance of infrastructure in regional development.

---

[7]   Leonardi (1993: 10).

[8]   John (1997) refers to Kent County as one of a few pioneer authorities of the 1980s that were successful in their application for structural funding, thereby promoting the development of networks between other county and regional authorities (John 1997: 134).

Traditionally, multi-level governance provided a theoretical tool for understanding the emergence of transnational ties between subnational authorities[9]. Goldsmith (1993) cites the driving forces between cross-border co-operation as being the increasing interdependence of the world economy, changes in the economic balance of power, shifts in location of industrial and manufacturing activities, increasingly important service and financial sectors, and dramatic changes in communication[10]. Transnational networks enhance the understanding of economic development issues and possibly improve policy responses with new innovative ideas.[11] Municipal competition and state restructuring are seen as the main incentives for the emergence of co-operative networks[12]. On the other hand, Ross (1994) recognises the importance of a specific functional focus for co-operation provided by infrastructure.[13] In the case of the Transmanche Euroregion, a high profile piece of infrastructure in the form of the Channel Tunnel and the Northern TGV network have provided the impetus for the promotion of trans-frontier networks.

The Channel Tunnel and associated high speed rail infrastructure provide a specific example of successful trans-frontier collaboration that could provide lessons pertaining to the emergence of subnational networks[14]. The participation of local authorities in functional policymaking related to high speed rail infrastructure promoted expanding networks between the local and regional actors. Transnational networks continued to grow, encouraged by the top-down support of the European Union. Economic trans-frontier regionalism provides a novel new input for local and regional authorities in the European policy-making process[15]. Understanding the interaction of subnational actors preparing for the impact of infrastructure provides an excellent focal point for describing the emergence and growth of transnational networks.

---

[9]   Marks (1996; 1997).

[10]   Goldsmith (1993).

[11]   Parkinson, Harding and Dawson (1994).

[12]   Cole and John (1995).

[13]   Ross (1994).

[14]   According to Brenner (1993) successful Inter-regional co-operation is characterised by the ability to consolidate the lines of progress in existence, bring about co-operation, match supply and demand, and develop a strategic outlook for such programmes in the medium and long term (Brenner, 1993: 244).

[15]   Bomberg and Peterson (1998).

Theoretical issues and framework

Multi-level governance and policy network theory have provided useful tools to describe the influence of subnational governments in European policy-making[16]. According to Rhodes (1981) central-local relations were seen as a 'game' in which the central and local authorities would manoeuvre for advantage[17]. Each of the actors deploying their resources to maximise their influence over policy outcomes. Rhodes and Marsh (1992) stressed the resources could be constitutional-legal, organisational, financial, political, or informational[18]. According to Heinelt and Smith (1996) it is a question of how in a multilevel system that is made up of the supranational EU level, the member states and the subnational level, political action can be co-ordinated and how such action can bring about the transformation of institutional structures[19].

Previous hierarchical relationships between European, national and subnational actors have given way to more complex structures with vertical and horizontal networks. Ansell Parsons and Darden (1997) provide an effective model for understanding the emergence of subnational networks that highlights the triangular relationship developing between the intergovernmental actors. They combine the insights of both multi-level governance authors and the "policy networks" literature, describing the triadic networks that connect supranational, national, and subnational actors as a form of multi-level governance. As suggested by the policy networks literature, these networks are built upon the exchange of resources in the form of information and technical assistance. However, many of the specific examples of political alliances are better characterised as the common opposition of two parties to a third party. While the result often appears to be an 'exchange' of political support, this exchange flows from the deeper structural logic of triadic relations[20].

The notion of "dual networks" occupies the space between policy networks and centre-periphery relationships. The changing nature of European governance has altered the manner in which central-local relationships are understood. No longer are central-local relationships understood by examining the interactions in a particular state. A broader scope is needed, taking into consideration the impact of trans-frontier

---

16   Marks (1997); Benington and Harvey (1998).
17   Rhodes (1981).
18   Rhodes and Marsh (1992).
19   Heinelt (1996: 9).
20   Ansell, Parsons, Darden (1997: 370).

co-operation. Thereby, accounting for transnational co-operation at a subnational level between local authorities in adjoining states, as well as with supranational institutions in the European Union. Further debate has surrounded policy networks as a useful analytical tool for understanding developments in the European Union[21]. What can be drawn from this debate over the nature of networks is that policy networks are based on resource dependency although the interpretations of the participants in policy networks tend to vary. Building on the policy network model, a "dual network" interpretation incorporates resource dependency, the expansion of centre-periphery relations and defines the intergovernmental actors in the field of European governance.

The "dual network" approach complements rather than contradicts the insights of both multilevel governance authors and the "policy networks" literature to which they often appeal. The approach combines the elements of intergovernmental relations that makes multilevel governance appealing with the descriptive abilities of policy networks. In addition the dual network approach incorporates "resource dependency" into its understanding, giving the heuristic device of policy networks the ability affect policy outcomes. It does not exclude micro-level transactions between public and private actors, nor does it ignore the macro-level policies of the European Union. Instead these are incorporated at a meso-level through and understanding of triadic networks, in which the supranational, national and subnational levels interact on the basis of resource dependencies.

Due to the diverse nature of subnational actors, identifying meso-regions is necessary in order to make a comparison between the central-local structures in various member states. Meso-regions are characterised by a relative spatial contiguity and may comprise regions which are 500 km to 800 km apart from one another. They are also to a certain extent based on a common identity, on reciprocal trust, and thus on a common sense of belonging; factors which represent a precondition to defining a common development strategy[22].

The actions of central governments and the European Union play an important role in determining meso-structures. Because central-local relations were structured by the *de jure* and *de facto* sovereignty of Parliament, the shift of decision-making and authority

---

[21]   Kenis and Schneider (1991).

[22]   Cappellin (1993: 2).

to the European level is likely to have important implications for the power and autonomy of local political institutions and other bodies. Whereas before 1973 central-local relations could, qualifications aside, be understood as a dyadic process involving a series of bargains carried out according to mainly centrally determined "rules of the game" between the two levels of governance, the new politics is best understood as a triadic game from which several possible outcomes on central-local politics can be inferred[23].

Institutional Framework and Meso-Levels

Two factors have contributed to the changes in intergovernmental relations; the first being state decentralisation, where power has been shifted from central government to subnational authorities, a key feature in West European countries since the 1970s. The other, European decentralisation through the Single European Market and the reform of the structural funds where movement away from the centre and towards the local governments was perceived as beneficial.[24] The exception to this rule is the United Kingdom, which has seen the rise of marketisation and consumerism and the centralising policies of *Margaret Thatcher*, where the concentration has been on privatisation[25]. The new forms of decentralisation can be discerned in the development of divergent forms of meso-regions in the participating nation-states.

The European Union constitutes an opportunity structure that offers additional resources to subnational governments. Increased resource dependency between tiers of governance and the public and the private sphere fosters the need for non-hierarchical patterns of interaction and co-ordination. Kohler-Koch (1996) emphasises this point, arguing that the EU does not only provide subnational actors with additional resources. The Commission provides a new philosophy of governance, based on co-operative governing, which changes the ideas and beliefs of subnational actors about how efficient governance can be achieved[26]. Subnational interests are mainly mobilised in functional niches around specific policy issues, usually with a European-wide span. They organise around supranational institutions, namely the European Commission and the European Parliament, as member state channels tend to be hostile. The European Commission plays an entrepreneurial role

---

[23]   John (1996: 294).

[24]   Goldsmith (1994).

[25]   See Stoker (1992) and Goldsmith (1992) who both refer to the role marketisation played in Britain.

[26]   Kohler-Koch (1996).

in shaping the functional niches, which are expected to spill over into other areas and from there into politics, gradually building an uninterrupted, and uniform, subnational political tier[27].

Further decentralisation as a result of the 1988 reform of the European structural funds encouraged subnational efforts to create networks outside of the traditional central-local structure.[28] The encouragement of networks by the European Commission provided local and regional authorities a greater range of options in addressing economic issues. Gradually, the Commission sought to increase its own influence over the framing and implementation of structural funds, converting them into a genuine instrument of regional policy. From the late 1980s, it also sought to co-opt regional interests as partners in designing and implementing programmes. This has produced a three-level contest for control of the policy instrument, among the Commission, member states and regions themselves[29]. In promoting the reform and development of the structural funds the Commission has opened up the possibility of direct contact between the European Union institutions and subnational officials.

In addition to a European-wide decentralisation through the reform of the structural funds, individual national efforts have supported decentralisation in participating member states[30]. Throughout most of the European Union the member-state governments have attempted to distribute power from the central government to local and regional authorities. The notable exception to this process has been the United Kingdom, which still demonstrates the resiliency of local and regional authorities in a European Single Market as County Councils become increasingly involved in the European arena[31]. Decentralisation has not diminished the role of the central government, but instead has acted to complement the aggregating role of member states. Hierarchical relationships are weak but interdependence is high. Actors are linked through networks, which span several levels and in which each actor contributes valuable resources[32]. Thus, decentralisation changed intergovernmental

---

[27]   Hooghe (1995: 196-197).

[28]   Hienelt and Smith (1996).

[29]   Keating (1998: 173).

[30]   The ability of central governments to remain the main interlocutor for regional development has been eroded during the last two decades due to the introduction of regional governments in a number of formally centralised states such as Italy, Belgium, France and Spain (Leonardi and Garmise, 1993: 269).

[31]   Bache, George and Rhodes (1996); Clark (1997).

[32]   Hooghe (1995: 178).

relationships from the hierarchical dominance of the central government to a series of vertical and horizontal networks in which various tiers of government interact.

The meso level in the United Kingdom is relatively weak in comparison to the rest of Western Europe, due in part to the disparity of relations between the centre and periphery. The reforms during the Thatcher years to reduce public expenditure resulted in frustrated local governments being overpowered by the centre[33]. Thus, resulting in the transition of the United Kingdom from a unitary state that was highly de-centralised to a unitary state which is highly centralised[34]. The British central-local structure is characterised by a dual polity in which there is little contact between the centre and periphery[35]. European trends towards decentralisation were reversed in Britain as the Thatcher government of the 1980s sought a market-based policy implemented by a strong central government. Reforms instituted by Thatcher were designed to increase the control of the central government over policy-making. Thus, organisations, such as the Greater London Council (GLC), which hampered the central efforts to control policy-making, were abolished. The strength of the centre and relative weakness of local authorities was characterised by Ashford (1982) as "British dogmatism". According to this description the powerful centre could pursue its own policy-making agenda without the constraints of consultation with subnational government[36]. This carried the bonus for the central government of achieving its policies more efficiently, however the detrimental aspect that emerged was derived from the lack of policy co-ordination between the centre and periphery. During the period between 1979 and 1990 Britain moved from being a welfare state to an enterprise one, resulting in a change in the role of local government from welfare producer and provider to reluctant enabler of market forces.[37] The literature on policy networks support this with examples of the growth of a tight central government in which the prime minister and ministers of the central government guided policy

---

[33]   Anderson (1990).

[34]   Jones (1988).

[35]   The term *dual polity* is derived from Bulpitt's (1983) work, where central government formulates the policy, and leaves the local government to implement legislation. Thereby creating a divide between centre and periphery in terms of policy-making (Bullpitt, 1983).

[36]   Ashford (1982).

[37]   Cochrane (1992).

towards a market ideology.[38] Thus, co-ordination between the centre and periphery has often been minimal, and as a result has called into question the existence of meso-level policy-making in Britain. Intra-regional bodies that exist in the United Kingdom have often been incapable of acting as an effective meso-level. Instead the county has been forced to fulfil the role of the meso-level in lieu of failed attempts at intra-regional co-operation in the United Kingdom. Increased pressure and responsibility associated with this new regional arrangement has forced the county to form networks with other actors in search of alternative sources of funding. This predicament was agitated by the reliance of the centre on market-oriented policies.

The evolution of French centre-periphery relations created a network structure that emphasised collaboration between central and local actors. Co-ordination previously took place under the guise of central control through *prefects* and *départments*, but was modified by reforms aimed at decentralisation[39]. Decentralisation reforms altered the influence of the regional councils and created a new network structure with the councils acting as a mediator between central and local actors. The restructuring manifested itself in the acquisition of European structural funds, which French regions were well equipped to pursue due to the collaborative nature of French central-local relations[40]. Thus, the regional council emerged as a new meso-level in French networks, institutionalising the collaborative networks that were characteristic of French public policy.

The development of regional authorities provided a new focus for understanding meso-level developments in France. Newly formed regional authorities developed

---

[38] Highlighting a micro-level approach to networks, Dudley and Richardson (1996) used policy networks to examine the operations of ministers and their relationships with departments. They found that ministers have mobility within their policy networks, meeting with a number of different actors. However, when it comes to policy implementation, the minister is able to ignore policy networks during implementation. This promiscuity gives the minister, and in turn the central government, greater power.

[39] As part of the Deferre reforms, the pre-existing regions, which had the legal status of *établissements publics*, would be strengthened by being upgraded to *collectivités territoriales* giving them power similar to the departments and municipalities and introducing democratically elected regional councils Loughlin and Mazey (1995; 1).

[40] In order to demonstrate the influence of structural funds in France, Lagrange (1997) examined the contributions from state planning contracts, *contrat de plan*, and European structural funds. He noted that the structural funds make up a significant portion of regional budgets, providing FF60 billion, thereby coming close to the states figure of FF75 billion in the period from 1994-1998 (Lagrange, 1997: 331).

into the principal meso-level. The regional structure was created with the functional requirements of economic development in mind. Thus, steps were taken in creating regional divisions to avoid confusion with traditional ethnic-regional identities. The administrative boundaries of the regional authorities were designed so that they did not coincide with historic regions. In doing this, the regional authorities could focus on administrative and economic modernisation. The regional authorities have continued to focus on these aims as essential to the development of their respective regions despite continued political development, leaving the French meso as essentially functional in its role[41].

Belgium has attempted to arrest ethnic divisions through the creation of a federal state, dividing competences between linguistic communities and regional parliaments[42]. The Belgium state underwent numerous stages of reform in an attempt to achieve a federal state. Recent reforms placed a great deal of power in the hands of the regional authority raising the spectre of regional autonomy and the threat of future devolution. The resulting structure is characterised as one of the strongest meso-level governments in Europe. The consequence of reform is a system in which the federal government attempts to maintain unity amongst regions which are continuously seeking new ways to further their autonomy.

Defining networks in Belgium is complicated by ongoing state reform[43]. Attempts to address policy networks in Belgium in the past have focused on the micro aspects of pillarisation and its relationship to neo-corporatism[44]. However, as the influence of the region in Belgian politics has increased, the application of a meso-level approach becomes increasingly workable. The influence of the region was recognised early on

---

[41]   Mazey (1993: 62-63).

[42]   Continuous reform of the Belgian federal structure has made a system which has been traditionally difficult to comprehend, even more complicated. The institutional reforms of 1970 put Belgium on the road towards a federal state. Instead of an partitioning Belgium into two federated states (Flanders and Wallonia), a more complex division into four linguistic territories (Dutch, French, German and bilingual) three regions (Flanders, Wallonia and Brussels) and three communities (Flemish, French and German) was elaborated. The principles of these institutional reforms were further developed in 1981, 1988-89 and 1993.

[43]   As Delmartino (1993) points out, "Anyone who is interested in the meso level in Belgium is therefore faced with the difficult task of identifying it." (Delmartino, 1993: 40).

[44]   See Van Den Bulck (1992) who argues that various forms of policy networks have acted to keep conflict within certain Belgian pillars allowing them to fester over time. Proof of this comes from Ethno-linguistic divisions which are not pillarised, and thus seem to be the only issue which threatens Belgian peace.

by Mughan (1985) who asserted that Belgium remains "all periphery and no centre". However, before a discussion can begin on politics in Belgium in terms of the centre-periphery model, some conceptual clarification is in order. Indeed, such a clarification is especially necessary in the specific context of Belgium, since no single perspective on centre-periphery relations is adequate for a full understanding of that country's political development and current structure of government[45]. Determining a centre-periphery relationship in Belgium is complicated by the construction of a federal state and the reform process. However, these two elements, which complicate the approach, have over time, served to clarify it in many respects. Efforts to maintain the integrity of the state while satisfying the desire for political autonomy in Belgium has led to a "regional federalism" which has created new centre-periphery relationships, in which the region has become a strong player in relation to the central government. Thus, since the reform process has involved the superimposition of a set of regional representative institutions on the traditional and highly centralised governmental structure, Belgium's current and incompletely articulated complex of representative institutions now embodies elements of both models of centre-periphery relations (geographic and urban/rural)[46]. Thus, the more Belgium has attempted to federalise, the more the characteristics resemble that of a unitary state, with centre-periphery co-operation and conflict between the regional governments and the central authority. More recent reforms in 1989 and 1993 bestowed upon the region a greater role in inter- or supranational forums by providing a larger and more coherent definition of their competences. Gradually the regions took advantage of the lack of clarity in the federal process in order to strengthen their position in the European forum. By stating that they had "implied power" the regions began to monopolise contact with the European Union, especially in areas effecting the preparation, decision-making and implementation of structural funds. This vigorous approach employed crucial resources such as formal competence, co-financing resources, and the personal skills of politicians and administrators and was successful in securing a strong negotiating position for the regions. Thus, the national government was reduced to the role of a "postman" in many instances[47]. Meanwhile, the regions were able to strengthen their connections with the European Union and the national

---

[45]   Mughan (1985: 273).
[46]   Mughan (1985: 276).
[47]   De Rynck (1996: 141).

164

governments of member states, and establish themselves as key actors in the distribution of structural funds[48].

An examination of the individual meso-levels in Britain, France and Belgium forms the foundation for understanding the reactions of local governments to infrastructure. Perspectives describing a French central-local relations characterise the Regional Council as the mediator between local authorities and the central government. Whereas Britain was characterised by a powerful personal form of governance relied on a strong central government and often neglected the periphery. Meanwhile constitutional reform of Belgian federalism altered the relationship between the central government and the regional authorities up until 1993. The dynamic nature of the centre-periphery relations in each nation created distinct environments for the conduct of local policy-making. Further enhanced by support from the European Union local policy-making altered as the local governments sought to expand their resources, and due to their national scenarios gain through co-operation with other localities. The manner in which localities pursue resources is largely dictated by the system which they inhabit. A case of "alienation" or "integration" appears to exist amongst the centre-periphery structures in the cross-channel area. The lack of resources and ultimately communication contributes to the need for local governments to seek those resources elsewhere. Prior to the emergence of a triangular approach to centre-periphery relations the localities would not have the option to seek resources through co-operation with the European Union and localities. The commonality between all three localities lay in the desire to find alternatives to the central government as a provider of resources.

The construction of high-speed rail infrastructure in preparation for the completion of the tunnel provides the clearest demonstration of differentiation in policy systems in the surrounding nations of Belgium, France and the United Kingdom. The United Kingdom witnessed the force of the central government over the protestation of the local. As the local government was wary of the preparation for infrastructure, the

---

[48] A pessimistic picture of regionalism in Belgium has been painted by Hooghe (1993). Moving from non-territorial to territorial organisation in Belgium in order to lessen inter-group contact has prevented conflict, but did little to diffuse separatist tendencies. Lack of incentives to co-operate and the desire for autonomy could result in further division of the Belgian political entity. Thus, the federal structure in an attempt to subdue ethno-regional conflict may have only displaced it as reforms have evolved from a complex federal structure gradually into a relationship based on regions, where the federal government is the weaker partner to the increasingly demanding regions. (Hooghe, 1993).

central government dictated the preparatory measures, relying on private enterprise and ultimately delaying the completion of the link until well after the opening of the tunnel. The French displayed the ability to plan long-term projects and prepare through co-operation between the central and local authorities. Using the pre-existing TGV system, SNCF officials, local government and central government co-ordinated to create a link between Lille and Calais which would best suit the area. In addition the planning for this link began soon after the tunnel project was approved. Whereas British and Belgian rails were still debating how to fund and construct the necessary links. Belgium, on the other hand, exhibited difficulties with regional autonomy as the regions quarrelled over the construction of the links. In comparison with Britain however, the central government was unable to push its agenda as regional autonomy dictated that Flanders and Wallonia determine what was to be done. Thus, the Belgian link was delayed as the regions fought over how the link was to be constructed.

Subnational Responses to Infrastructure

The role played by subnational authorities, from the initial meetings to the eventual agreement to form the Transmanche Euroregion, mirrored the growing influence of a third-level in the European Union. The impetus to build the Channel Tunnel and associated infrastructure was mandated by the central governments of Britain and France.[49] Gradually, as the functional obligation to address the problems associated with the fixed link arose, the subnational governments became increasingly influential. Additional factors, such as the creation of the Single Market and reform of the structural funds, provided subnational authorities with new resources for developing their autonomy. In addition tackling functional problems, such as the employment difficulties created by the tunnel, required cross-border co-ordination on issues better suited to the local and regional authorities of the participating member states. Bottom-up initiatives on the part of local and regional authorities resulted in the emergence of an innovative form of transfrontier governance that embodies a significant element of subnational mobilisation in the European Union.

The distinct difference between the French, British and Belgian centre-periphery relations, and how their arrangement affected policy-making in relation to high speed rail infrastructure becomes increasingly evident throughout the history of the trans-frontier region. As the short term effects of the tunnel were centred on the cross-

---

[49]   Gibb (1994).

Channel region, the long term effects involved a larger geographical area. The creation of a Trans-European Network structure required the linking of the major European capitals. The focus point of this link was the Paris-London-Brussels route. Linking the capitol cities required changes in the infrastructure designed to accommodate the increased high speed rail traffic that would evolve from the completion of a fixed link. The preparedness of the three member states and how their internal structures managed in developing a high speed rail system to suit the tunnel is indicative of the lack of central-local co-ordination in the British system, the comparatively comprehensive co-ordination of the French system, and the growing desire for local autonomy in the Belgian system.

The high speed rail link saga in the UK illustrates the difficulties of long term strategic planning with a market-led approach to transport investment[50]. A key variance between the central and local governments over the Channel Tunnel was the difference in opinion over the amount of preparation required. Initially the central government was unwilling to invest in the South East, and felt that there was no need for investing in high-speed rail infrastructure. Instead the emphasis was placed on a market led approach and the high speed rail link was offered as a concession. The Select Committee of the House of Commons on the Channel Tunnel Bill (1986) did not believe intervention was necessary to protect the poorer parts of the region on the grounds that investment from the tunnel could bypass the localities and end up in London[51]. However, from the perspective of Kent County Council the Channel Tunnel linked a depressed industrial region, Nord Pas de Calais, where development grants and state inducements are available, to the South East of the United Kingdom, an area which lacked a great deal of central support[52]. Thus, Kent perceived itself at a disadvantage to its French counterparts in attracting industry and businesses investment. The lack of central support, embodied in the delay in the construction of a high-speed rail link, forced the county council in Kent to pursue new resources in anticipating the impact of the Channel Tunnel. In an effort to fund projects designed to assist with the long term and short-term impact the local authority pursued networks with cross-Channel counterparts. Thus, Kent became a willing partner and

---

[50]   Gibb and Knowles (1994: 197).

[51]   "We have heard evidence of the pockets of high unemployment in Thanet and the fears of many people in Dover about the effect of the Tunnel. Nevertheless, we do not think it right to require the government to adopt specific policies on economic assistance to this part of Kent purely as a consequence of the Tunnel project." House of Commons (1986).

[52]   Gibb (1985: 347).

the equivalent of a meso-level in Britain in order to acquire the resources required to support its pro-active fixed link policy-making.

The existence of consultative networks and the access of local governments to national and European officials imbued the Regional Council of Nord Pas de Calais with the ability to take a pro-active approach to the construction of high speed rail infrastructure. The outcome of co-ordinated policy-making in regard to high-speed rail developments was the EuraLille project, which was designed to take advantage of Lille's emerging status as a crossroads of Europe. Crucial to the development of EuraLille was the decision to build the Paris London rail link through Lille, creating a junction for a Paris Brussels route. The junction of these new high-speed lines was initially due to have been some 10km out of Lille, however Lille mayor, **Pierre Mauroy**, used his influence as Socialist prime minister to ensure both that the junction was in the centre of the city, and the construction of an underground station could be funded through public money[53]. As Van Staeyen (1996) points out, the border, and the Lille's location on the border determined the development of the city and its metropolitan area. The border areas surrounding Lille promoted a greater degree of cross-border co-operation. As a result, urban areas on both sides of the border in Flanders, Wallonia and France saw their future development in terms of a cross border perspective, collaborating on a metropolitan area that straddles the Franco-Belgian border[54]. The ability of Nord Pas de Calais to capitalise on the Channel Tunnel and associated infrastructure was illustrated by the success of EuraLille and the emergence of Lille as a crossroads in the European transport network. The access of the region to national and European officials, as well as the role it played as an adept meso-level co-ordinator, placed Nord Pas de Calais in a prime position to be the lynch-pin of the Transmanche Euroregion. The Regional Council of Nord Pas de Calais demonstrated an adept ability to pursue and acquire funding. However, the funding required to address massive changes in infrastructure and industry demanded alternative sources of funding. In addition to addressing cross-national issues related to infrastructure, co-operation with localities across the border provided Nord Pas de Calais with access to expanded resources.

---

[53]   Pierre Mauroy, who was Prime Minister at the time, acted as a crucial link between central and local authorities. In addition to his role as Prime Minister Mauroy, under the premise of *cumul des mandats*, held the position of Mayor of Lille and was undoubtedly the leading politician in Nord Pas de Calais Knapp (1991).

[54]   Van Staeyen (1996).

Belgian attempts to construct a high-speed line demonstrate the complexity of the Belgian federal model, while highlighting the growing regional clout in Belgian policy-making. The incessant delays in the creation of a high speed rail network necessary to form part of the Trans-European networks were related to the difficulties faced by SNCB/NMBS and the central government in negotiating with the regions of Wallonia, Flanders and Brussels Capital. The ability of the regions to complicate and slow down the building of the high-speed network was indicative of a federal system in which the regions maintained a powerful influence. The ability of the central government to influence planning of the rail network was inhibited by the relationship between the regions, and the continuing desire of Flanders and Wallonia to assert some degree of autonomy. Wallonia, which was traditionally agricultural, feared the high-speed network would create a corridor effect leaving the Walloons on the periphery, far from the benefits of a high speed rail network. Flanders also feared a peripheral status, however the construction of a high-speed rail network posed a new set of problems for the region. The dense population of Flanders made construction of a high-speed rail network difficult. In order to address these difficulties Flanders, Wallonia and the Belgian federal government negotiated a compromise over the construction of the infrastructure network. Delays caused by regional resistance cost the national rail company, under the control of the federal government, and threatened to bring the high speed rail project to a halt. Attempts by the federal government to expedite negotiations were met with a stalemate between the two regions. Eventually the regions agreed to the construction of new infrastructure in Wallonia and the upgrading of old infrastructure in Flanders.[55] The agreed upon approach was not the most practical in terms of direct high-speed rail construction, however it served to fulfil the needs of the regions. The central government and SNCB were unable to dictate the manner in which the network was constructed, but had to rely on consultation. However unlike central-local consultation in France, conflict between the regions inhibited construction. This ongoing desire on the part of Belgian regions to assert autonomy made them amiable to seeking resources from other actors than their own federal government.

Wallonia, Flanders and Brussels Capital have developed divergent positions on intervention, which was evident in their approach to the development of high-speed rail. Particularly in Wallonia and Flanders, between which a certain amount of regional tension exists. The pro-intervention Walloons, sought to increase investment

---

[55]   Southey, (1995).

in the area through the construction of infrastructure and have followed through on this model by promoting cross-border partnerships that could bring in funding.[56] Flanders, on the other hand, objected to state intervention and restricted rail infrastructure to rail lines that were previously constructed. Flanders' desire to distance themselves from the Wallonia and the Belgian state structure has promoted Flemish involvement in cross-border co-operative arrangements.[57] Thus, although the regions may have divergent regional structures and political ideologies, they seem to have converged on functional issues related to spatial planning, funding, and developing regional autonomy.

In comparison to the British county, the Belgian regions were highly involved with the policy-making process in relation to the creation of transport infrastructure. The federal structure of Belgium granted the regions with planning power and input into the procedures related to infrastructure development. However, unlike the French, the access of the regions to the central government did not necessarily ensure co-operation and co-ordination. The desire on the part of Belgian regions to increase their autonomy led to conflict between the regions. Thus, the preparation resulting from co-ordination seen in France was not as visible in Belgium. In-fighting between the regions in regard to financing and construction of a high speed network resulted in delays in the completion of the route. Thus, although the Belgian federal system was designed to promote co-operation between the centre-periphery, as in the French system, the construction of a high speed rail network had the characteristics of the British centre-periphery disparity.

The Transmanche Euroregion developed out of initial contact between Kent and Nord Pas de Calais over the Channel Tunnel. Attempts by the subnational governments to anticipate problems created by the fixed link initiated a number of meetings between the local authorities. The meetings were initiated by Kent, which felt that the central government of the UK had done little to prepare for the externalities which might develop. Informal meetings between local officials were initially successful and led to further meetings being scheduled between the localities. This in turn led to the scheduling of regular meetings designed to co-ordinate policy between the local officials. In these meetings the Transfrontier Development Programme (TDP) was initiated to structure the cross-border co-operation between the localities.

---

[56]   Quevit and Bodson (1993).
[57]   De Rynck and De Rynck (1996).

Developments in the European Union expanded the benefits of cross-border co-operation through the Interreg programme. This, coupled with the success of the TDP led to the signing of the Transmanche agreement between Kent and Calais, thereby creating an European Economic Interest Group (EEIG). At that time, cross-border co-operation between French and Belgian authorities over the Lille metropolis was also developing. Belgian plans to create high speed infrastructure to accommodate the TENS and the Tunnel led to further co-operation on the part of the localities. Continued success for the Transmanche region as a regional voice in European affairs led the regions of Belgium to seek inclusion into the agreement. Thus, the Transmanche region was expanded to include the regions of Wallonia, Flanders and Brussels Capital and expanded the area into what is now know as the Transmanche Euroregion. As well, the powers, meeting times, and topics of co-ordination were also expanded in the development of the Transmanche Euroregion.

Conclusion

The Transmanche Euroregion was based on regular meetings between local officials. Thus, the current structure of the Euroregion still relies on meetings between local officials. In the meetings local officials co-ordinate policies with one another, trade ideas for development and employ local development strategies. The core of the Euroregion consists of a "college of members", which is administrated by a Secretariat. At present the "college of members" consists of representatives from each of the five member regions. The representative is usually a European officer who works in conjunction with their local authority. Co-ordination between the localities is divided into five working groups. The groups include infrastructure development, economic development, trade and training, environment, and tourism. All of these spread across national boundaries and deal with topics that have become increasingly part of the policy realm of local government.

The majority of the Euroregions efforts towards co-operation concentrate on economic development and the improvement of infrastructure. This is closely linked to the initial impetus for the creation of the Euroregion, based on co-operation over the development of cross-Channel infrastructure. The region published a series of themes and actions to clarify the topics of co-operation and provide the organisation with more focus[58]. The focus was further defined through a seminar held in Brussels in

---

[58]   Euroregion Strategic Planning and Infrastructure Group (1994).

1994. It was also agreed to produce a collection of statistics based on the Euroregion to give policy-makers a guide for policy co-ordination. As it stands the Euroregion has no binding influence on the localities, but simply acts as a forum for co-operation between the localities.

The contribution of the European Union to the emergence of the Euroregion across the English Channel is closely linked to the funding opportunities offered to the subnational authorities. Community Initiatives, brought about by the reform of the structural funds promoted the development of networks between local authorities. The most influential of these programmes in terms of cross-border networks was the Interreg programme, which was designed to assist frontier regions. In addition to developing horizontal networks, the funds were also instrumental in promoting the foundation of links between the subnational authorities and European Union officials.

Although transport infrastructure was a prominent motor for integration, the impetus for the emergence of the Transmanche Euroregion cannot solely be placed on the Channel Tunnel and the Single European Market. Bottom-up integration comes into play in understanding cross-channel developments. The desire on the part of local authorities to expand their abilities to make policy combined with the European need to access information without the cumbersome mediator of the nation state aided the development of Euroregions as a whole. Further impetus for transnational co-operation was brought on by the situations localities found themselves in due to their perceived domestic centre-periphery difficulties. In the specific case of the Channel Tunnel infrastructure, changing sources of resource dependency coupled with a need to influence policy-making resulted in a strengthening of European-local ties. The opportunism of the participating regions is noteworthy, taking advantage of the structure of the European Union to further regional autonomy by accessing funding and actively supporting regional development in the European Union.

The issues covered by the focus of the Euroregion tend to operate in areas where local and regional government would normally influence policy-making and thus do little to enhance the powers of local government. Areas such as transport, the environment, spatial planning and employment, have traditionally fallen under the remit of local government. The difference in the development of the Euroregion is that the local government now has the information and therefore the ability to plan over a wider area in relation to the aforementioned issues. Thus, the power of local governments to input on the issues or make autonomous decisions has not happened to the extent that the Euroregion has become its own polity, however, the regional authorities are better equipped to address trans-national issues. In addition, contact with European institutions has provided local governments an opportunity to voice opinions, exchange information and access resources. However the altered relationship between local, national and European government, does not ensure autonomy for local government or the creation of a Europe of the regions. Nor does local-European contact necessarily take from the power of the centre in each member state to maintain control over localities. Instead a new relationship appears to have developed between the three tiers of government altering the manner in which they interact with one another. The change in balance between local, national and European gives local government more choices in the form of resources, however it does not necessarily remove power from the national governments. The developments in local, national, European relationships points more towards a growing complexity than it does to a loss of sovereignty.

Contrary to the fear of "bypassing the nation-state" the Euroregion has become an added element in the complex networks that make up policy-making at the local-level in the EU. The Euroregion has evolved from several factors including resource dependency and regional competition, Functional partnership through bottom-up initiatives, and decentralisation embodied in the top down approaches adopted by national governments and the European Union. The significant factor in the emergence of the Transmanche Euroregion appears to be the role played by infrastructure in acting as a catalyst for advancing networks. The Channel Tunnel and associated infrastructure provided a forum for subnational authorities to build networks that expanded and formed the Transmanche Euroregion.

Bibliography

Alomar, Susana Borras, (1995), "Interregional Co-operation in Europe during the Eighties and Early Nineties" in Soerensen, Nils Arne (ed.) *European Identities: Cultural Diversity and Integration in Europe since 1700*, Odense University Press, 127-46.

Anderson, Jeffery, J., (1990), "When Market and Territory Collide: Thatcherism and the politics of regional decline", *West European Politics*, Vol 13, April 1990, No. 2, pp. 234-257.

Ansell, C.K., Parsons, C., and Darden, K., (1997), "Dual Networks in European regional development policy.", *Journal of Common Market Studies*, 35 (3) September 97, pp. 347-75.

Ashford, D., (1982), *British Dogmatism and French Pragmatism: Central-Local Policymaking in the Welfare State,* Allen & Unwin, London, 1982.

Bache, I., George, S. and Rhodes, R.A.W., (1996), "The European Union, Cohesion Policy and Subnational Authorities in the United Kingdom", in Hooghe, Liesbet (ed), *Cohesion policy and European integration: building multi-level governance*, Oxford; Oxford University Press, 1996.

Benington, J. and Harvey J., (1998), "Transnational local authority networking within the European Union: passing fashion or new paradigm" in Marsh, David (ed), *Comparing Policy Networks*, Open University Press.

Bomberg, E. and Peterson, J., (1998), "European Union Decision Making: the Role of Sub-national Authorities", *Political Studies*, Volume 46, No. 2, June 1998, pp. 219-235.

Bradbury, J. and Mawson, J., (1997), *British Regionalism and Devolution*, Athenaeum Press, Gateshead, Tyne and Wear.

Brenner, P., (1993), "What makes an Interregional Network Successful", in Cappellin, R. and Batey, P.W. (eds), *Regional Networks, Border Regions and European Integration*, London: Pion.

Brunt, Barry M., (1995), "Regions and Western Europe", *Journal of Geography*, January/February 1995, Volume 94, No. 1.

Bullpitt, J.G., (1983), *Territory and Power in the United Kingdom*, Manchester; Manchester University Press, 1983.

Cappellin, R., (1993), "Interregional Co-operation in Europe: An Introduction" in Cappellin, R. and Batey, P.W. (eds), *Regional Networks, Border Regions and European Integration*, London: Pion.

Cappellin, R. and Batey, P.W. (eds), (1993), *Regional Networks, Border Regions and European Integration,* London: Pion.

Clark, D., (1997), "Local government in Europe: retrenchment, restructuring and British exceptionalism", *West European Politics*, 20 (3), July 1997, pp. 134-163.

Cochrane, A., (1992), "The changing state of local government: restructuring for the 1990's", *Public Administration*, 69, pp. 281-302.

Cole A., and John P., (1995), "Models of Local Decision-Making Networks in Britain and France", *Policy and Politics,* October, 1995, Vol 23, no. 4 303.

Delmartino, (1993), "Belgium: In Search of the Meso Level", in Sharpe (ed), *The Rise of Meso Government in Europe*, SAGE Publications, 1993.

De Rynck, S., (1996), "Europe and Cohesion Policy-Making in the Flemish Region" in Hooghe, L., (ed.), *Cohesion Policy and European Integration: Building Multi-Level Governance*, Oxford: Oxford University Press, pp. 129-162.

De Rynck, S., (1997), "Belgian Local Government: Far Away from Brussels", in Goldsmith, M.J.F. and K. K. Klausen, *European Integration and Local Government*, Edward Elgar, Cheltenham, 1997.

De Rynck, F. and De Rynck, S., (1996), "The Implementation of Structural Funds Programmes in the Flemish Region", in Hesse, J.J. and Toneen, A,J. (ed.) *The European Yearbook of Comparative Government and Public Administration*, Westview Press, Boulder, Colorado.

Dudley, G. and J. Richardson, (1996), "Promiscuous and celibate ministerial styles: policy change, policy networks and British roads policy", *Parliamentary Affairs*, 49 (4), Oct 1996, pp. 566-583.

Euroregion Strategic Planning and Infrastructure Group, (1994), *'A Vision for Euroregion': Towards a Policy Framework*, Euroregion, Brussels, 1994, p.3.

Gibb, R., (ed.), (1994), *The Channel Tunnel: A Geographical Perspective*. Wiley: August 1994.

Gibb, R., and Knowles, R., (1994), *The High-speed Rail Link: Planning and Development Implications*, in Gibb, Richard (ed.), 1994. *The Channel Tunnel: A Geographical Perspective*. Wiley: August 1994.

Goldsmith, M., (1992), "Local government", *Urban Studies*, Vol. 29, 1992, pp. 393-410.

Goldsmith, M., (1993), "The internationalisation of local authority policy", *Urban Studies*, Vol. 30, 1993, pp. 683-708.

Goldsmith, M., (1994), "The Europeanisation of Local Government", *Urban Studies*, Vol. 29, 1994, pp.393-410.

Heinelt, H. and Smith, R., (1996), *Policy Networks and European Structural Funds*, Avesbury, Suffolk.

Hooghe, L., (1993) "Belgium: from regionalism to federalism", *Regional Politics & Policy*, 3(1), Spring 1993, pp. 44-68.

Hooghe, L., (1995), "Belgian Federalism and the European Community", in Jones, B. and Keating, M., *The European Union and the Regions*, Clarendon Press Oxford.

House of Commons, (1986), *Great Britain. House of Commons. Select Committee on the Channel Tunnel Bill. Special report from the session 1986-87, together with appendices and the proceedings of the Committee*, H M Stationery Office, Bernan/UNIPUB: 1986.

John, P., (1996), "Centralization, decentralization and the European Union: the dynamics of triadic relationships.", *Public Administration*, 74 (2) Summer 96, pp. 293-313.

John, P., (1997), "Europeanisation in a Centralising State: Multi-level Governance in the UK", in Jeffery, Charlie (ed.), *The Regional Dimension of the European Union, Towards a Third Level in Europe?*, Frank Cass, London.

Jones, G., (1988), "The crisis in British central-local government relationships", *Governance*, 1 (2), April 1988, pp. 162-183.

Keating, M., (1993a), "The politics of economic development", *Urban Affairs*, Quarterly, 28, pp. 373-396.

Keating, M., (1993b), "The Continental Meso: Regions in the European Community", in Sharpe (ed), *The Rise of Meso Government in Europe*, SAGE Publications.

Keating, M., (1998), *The New Regionalism in Western Europe*, Edward Elgar, Cheltenham, UK.

Kenis, P. and Schneider, V., (1991), "Policy networks and policy analysis: scrutinising a new analytical toolbox", in Marin and Mayntz, (eds), *Policy Network: Empirical Evidence and Theoretical Considerations*, Frankfurt am Main: Campus Verlag.

Knapp, A., (1991), "The cumul des mandates, local power and political parties in France", *West European Politics*, 14 (1), Jan 1991, pp. 18-40.

Kohler-Koch, B., (1996), "The Strength of Weakness: the Transformation of Governance in the EU" in Gustavsson S. and Lewin, L., (eds), *The Future of the Nation State*, Stockholm, Nerius & Santerus, 169-210, 1996.

Lagrange, R., (1997), "French Policy Perspectives", in Bachtler, John and Ivan Turok, *The Coherence of EU Regional Policy; contrasting perspectives on Structural Funds*, Athenaeum Press, Gateshead, Tyne and Wear.

Leonardi, R., (1993), "The Role of Subnational Institutions in European Integration", in Leonardi (ed.), 1993, *The Regions and the European Community: The Regional Response to the SingleMarket in the Underdeveloped Areas*, Frank Cass, 1993

Leonardi, R., and Garmise, S., (1993), "Subnational Elites and the European Community", in Leonardi (ed.), *The Regions and the European Community: The Regional Response to the SingleMarket in the Underdeveloped Areas*, Frank Cass.

Loughlin, J., and Mazey, S., (1995), *The End of the French Unitary State?*, Frank Cass, London.

Marks, G., (1996), "Exploring and Explaining Variation in Cohesion Policy", in Hooghe, L. (ed.), *Cohesion Policy and European Integration: Building Multi-level Governance*, Oxford: Oxford University Press.

Marks, G., (1997), "An Actor-Centred Approach to Multi-Level Governance Studies", in Jeffery, Charlie (ed.), *The Regional Dimension of the European Union, Towards a Third Level in Europe?*, Frank Cass, London.

Marsh, D. and Rhodes, R., (1992), "Policy Communities and Issue Networks. Beyond Typology", in Marsh, D., and Rhodes, R., (eds.), *Policy Networks in British Government,* Oxford: Clarendon Press, pp. 249-268.

Mazey, S., (1993), "Developments at the French Meso Level: Modernizing the French State", in Sharpe (ed), *The Rise of Meso Government in Europe*, SAGE Publications.

Mughan, A., (1985), "Belgium: All Periphery and No Centre?", in Mény, Y., and Wright, V., *Centre Periphery Relations in Western Europe*, London, Gerorge Allen & Unwin.

Parkinson, M., Harding, A. and Dawson, J., (1994), "The changing face of urban Europe" in A. Harding, J. Dawson, et al. (eds), *European Cities Towards 2000*, pp. 1-16. Manchester: Manchester University Press.

Quévit, M. and Bodson, S., (1993), "Transborder Co-operation and European Integration: The Case of Wallonia", in Cappellin, R. and Batey, P.W. (eds), *Regional Networks, Border Regions and European Integration,* London: Pion.

Rhodes, R., (1981), *Control and Power in Central-Local Government Relations.* Farnborough: Gower.

Ross, J., (1994), "High speed rail: catalyst for European integration?", *Journal of Common Market Studies*, 32 (2), June 1994, pp. 191-214.

Scott, J., (1999a), *Comprehending Transboundary Regionalism: Developing an Analytical Domain for Comparative Research*, RSA International Conference, 1999.

Scott, J., (1999b), "European and North American Contexts for Cross-Border Regionalism", *Regional Studies*, 33(7), pp. 605-617.

Sem Fure, J., (1997), "The German-Polish Border Region. A Case of Regional Integration?", *Arena Working Papers*, WP 97/19, http://www.sv.uio.no/arena/publications/wp97_19.htm.

Sharpe, L. J., (1993a), "The European Meso: an Appraisal" in L. J. Sharpe (ed), *The Rise of Meso Government in Europe*, London: Sage Publications, 1993.

Sharpe, L. J.,(1993b), "The United Kingdom: The Disjointed Meso", in Sharpe (ed), *The Rise of Meso Government in Europe*, SAGE Publications.

Smith. A., (1997), "Studying Multi-level Governance examples from French translations of structural funds", *Public Administration*, Vol. 75 Winter 1997, pp 711-729.

Southey, C., (1995), "Controversy Threatens Rail Network", *Financial Times*, Special Report on Belgium, 28 June, 1995.

Stoker, G., (1992), *The Politics of Local Government*, 2nd ed. London: Macmillan.

Thompson, I., (1994), "The French TGV System: Progress and Projects", *Geography*, No. 343, Vol. 79 Part 2, April 1994.

Van Der Veen, A., (1993), "Theory and Practice of Cross-border Co-operation of Local Governments: The Case of the EUREGIO between Germany and the Netherlands", in Cappellin, R. and Batey, P.W. (eds), *Regional Networks, Border Regions and European Integration*, London: Pion.

Van Staeyen, J., (1996), "Lille as a European Metropolis: a metropolitan policy in a cross-border region", Agence de développement et d'ubanisme de la métropole lilloise, JVS 30 April 1996 speech for the Conference on "Socio-economic development and democracy - towards an institutional model", Trencin, Slovakia.

Vickerman, R. W., (1989), "Measuring changes in regional competitiveness: the effects of international infrastructure investments.", *Annals of Regional Science*, 23:275-86 No. 4.

Weyand, S., (1997), "Inter-regional Associations and the European Integration Process", in Jeffery, C., (ed.), *The Regional Dimension of the European Union, Towards a Third Level in Europe?*, Frank Cass, London.

2002/2003

THE ROLE OF REGIONS AND CITIES IN THE INTEGRATION OF THE CANDIDATE COUNTRIES: EVALUATION AND PERSPECTIVES

Chair of the Selection Board

Mr Luis Durnwalder, head of government of South Tyrol.

Theses submitted

NUMBER OF ENTRANTS	LANGUAGES		COUNTRY	
10	5	German English Spanish French Portuguese	7	Germany Austria Spain France Ireland Portugal Sweden

Winners:

First prize:

Mr Georges Mercier (FR), *Regional Development in Slovakia and European Integration*, Université Pierre Mendès France, Grenoble

Second prize:

Dr Patricia Schläger-Zirlik (DE), *The learning region strategy in urban and regional development*, University of Bayreuth

Georges Mercier, Université Pierre Mendès France

Regional Development in Slovakia and European Integration

This article is drawn from a thesis on Regional Development in Slovakia and European Integration. The aim of this thesis was to highlight the way in which the countries of central and eastern Europe are now trying, under a strong European influence, to reposition themselves on the field of regional development.

Looking back on this work, we hope first of all to list the main issues raised by the application of Europe's political structure to the CEEC over the last few years. Secondly, we also offer some comments on the recent guidelines adopted by the Member States and the Commission in this area at a time when ten new countries are about to join the EU.

Introduction

When the Berlin Wall fell in November 1989, it was the start of a new era in European history. The countries of "Eastern Europe" regained their independence and fundamentally reconsidered their political directions and their development strategies. Faced with significant economic difficulties and with the need to reorganise their political and institutional systems, and seeking international recognition, these countries turned resolutely to the West during the 1990s.

However, their rapid progress towards EU membership requires them to comply with a number of constraints that leave the political elites and the population little time to absorb the shock of transition. The strategic decisions that are being taken on economic, social and territorial policy will nonetheless have a significant effect on the future of these countries beyond the advantages that EU enlargement will bring.

The question that must now be asked is whether the choices made in the haste to accede to the EU will be the best ones to carry forward the (economic and social) development policies appropriate to each of them in the long term. At the same time, the budgetary constraints of the Union and the guidelines adopted at the European

Councils of Lisbon and Gothenburg will significantly affect regional policy for the countries of central and eastern Europe.

Our aim in this context is to put the choices made into perspective and to question whether they were appropriate to the expectations and the particular environment in which the new members find themselves.

What kind of regional policy is appropriate for the countries of central and eastern Europe?

All the countries of central and eastern Europe submitted their applications for EU entry in the mid-1990s. The EU responded favourable by launching an ambitious pre-accession process. The first few years of reform were characterised by the creation of the PHARE assistance programme and the signing of Europe agreements that were essentially aimed at promoting the installation of democratic regimes and market economies in these countries. The first transition phase was marked by waves of privatisation, the opening up of the markets, and a rapid restructuring of the economy.

The issues of territorial cohesion initially received relatively little attention due to the macroeconomic constraints and the lack of organisation within the political/administrative system. The priority in the early 1990s was to make the structural adjustments that were necessary to reflect the overturning of the economic model that had characterised the previous regime.

Nonetheless, those in authority quickly became aware of the socio-economic consequences of the reforms that were taking place. The collapse of entire sectors of industry, the end of most state subsidies, and the lack of organisation in agriculture meant that some regions were severely affected by the crisis. Rural areas away from the main arteries of communication, and medium-sized, single-industry towns, were the worst affected, with unemployment rates exceeding 30%.

As a result of budgetary restrictions and a sweeping rejection of the methods and tools of intervention used in central planning, these countries had limited scope for action and initially relied on the free market to offset the recession that was affecting the most fragile regions.

At the same time, the European Union set out the content of the pre-accession process, by the end of which the candidate countries had to satisfy the *Copenhagen criteria* and comply with the various requirements of the *partnership for accession.*

Economic aid is progressively steering the countries of eastern and central Europe towards assistance mechanisms that have been tested over many years within the EU and are supported by specific funds (Structural Funds and Cohesion Funds). The aid policy that was put in place at the end of the 1990s, and fleshed out in 2000 by access to the ISPA[1] and SAPARD[2] pre-accession funds, thus aims both to promote economic growth in struggling areas and to familiarise the countries of central and eastern Europe with EU-specific programming and intervention methods.

However, as we have been able to demonstrate in the case of Slovakia, the European Commission's approach came up against a number of difficulties[3].

First of all, it should be noted that European regional or structural policy has developed since the late 1950s as successive enlargements have taken place. Each accession provided an opportunity for the candidate countries to have existing policy changed in order to take into consideration the particular economic, geographical or social constraints.

In 1973, the United Kingdom, which was a candidate for EEC membership along with Denmark and Ireland, negotiated not to be a net contributor to the European budget immediately upon entry. As it was unable to benefit from the CAP[4] due to its agricultural sector being insufficiently large, the country wanted "compensation" for the restructuring of its crisis-hit industry. The result was the creation, on 18 March 1975, of the European Regional Development Fund (ERDF), which was aimed at financing infrastructure projects and industrial investment in deprived areas.

In order to assist European fruit and vegetable-producing regions that might be affected by the accession of Greece in 1981, followed by that of Spain and Portugal in 1986, *Integrated Mediterranean Programmes* were introduced in 1985.

---

[1]   ISPA: Instrument for structural policy for pre-accession
[2]   SAPARD: Special Accession Programme for Agriculture and Rural Development
[3]   Georges Mercier, *Développement régional en Slovaquie et intégration européenne*, Institut d'Urbanisme de Grenoble, December 2002.
[4]   CAP: Common Agricultural Policy

Finally, in 1995, the accession of Sweden and Finland led to the creation of a specific priority objective aimed at very sparsely populated regions, Objective 6, which was replaced by Objective 1 after 1999.

European structural policy is therefore the result of continual negotiations between countries that are aware both of their political assets and of the aspects of their economies that will enable them to access new kinds of financing.

The situation in the countries of central and eastern Europe is somewhat different for the following reasons. At a political level, these countries approached the EU as a disparate group, with each one of them wishing to appear as the most westernised of the accession countries. The desire to pass the accession exam pushed the candidate countries further towards accepting the constraints imposed by the EU. Despite strong views, such as that of Poland regarding the Common Agricultural Policy[5], the accession negotiations did not give rise to very specific demands in the area of regional policy.

This situation was doubtless exacerbated by the tough context of political and economic reforms, which prevented the countries of central and eastern Europe from putting together clear, formal strategies in this area. The countries of eastern and central Europe had, in fact, to adapt their legislation, their institutions and their management methods to a system of financing that had been developed by and for countries that had for several decades been used to territorial planning and development measures.

This adaptation was reflected by the creation, often from scratch, of ministries for regional development or of departments within the ministries of the economy, the environment, or the Prime Minister's office. With limited resources and very little time, these bodies had to draw up *National Plans for Regional Development*, the intitial planning documents with a view to receiving Structural Fund financing. Within the same timeframe, the EU required the creation of management and payment authorities for future sectoral and regional operational programmes.

At the territorial level, the need to introduce "programming regions" affected the debate on the devolution process. The desire expressed by the Commission to give regions responsibility in drawing up programmes and implementing the Structural Funds was at

---

[5]   CAP funding for the new members will be phased in (25% in 2004, 30% in 2005, and so on). Poland opposed this phased integration, but was not able to alter the EU's position significantly.

times perceived as a strong encouragement to create devolved regions. Faced with this pressure, Slovakia took less than two years to establish new administrative areas and create regional councils. When one considers the way in which the devolution process in Europe has developed, often over several decades, it is legitimate to ask what the consequences will be of these hurried reforms in the short, medium and long term.

Once these structures have been created, the issue arises as to the human and financial resources available to them to accomplish their new tasks. The difficulty for the authorities, apart from budget constraints, is to draw up programmes for action in an area where professional knowledge and experience are not yet adequate.

If these countries are fully to reclaim the field of local and regional politics, they must first rebuild a territorial culture beyond the requirements set out by the European Commission. This includes government support for university courses, which are trying to adapt their curricula in the areas of town and country planning, local and regional administration, regional economy, etc. This is key to the ability of actors to come up with effective long-term development strategies.

The lack of human resources and low levels of co-financing have made it difficult for local authorities to put together projects or put forward viable proposals to the European Commission. In addition to this limited capacity to use available funds, there has been an added difficulty in directing finance to the areas that need it most. Apart from the equipment programmes, which will need many more years of investment (infrastructure, environment), territorial development projects proper have a tendency to be concentrated in areas that have the greatest capacity for financing and innovation (in the most heavily urbanised and most dynamic areas).

Faced with this situation, the European Commission has sought to simplify and refocus its territorial development aid policy in central Europe. The first effect of this was a redrawing of the programming areas in favour of very large regions within countries. The idea was to limit the number of management, monitoring and control authorities, which led, in the Visegrad group countries[6], to the creation of Community Support

---

[6] This group consists of Poland, the Czech Republic, Slovakia and Hungary. Its aim is to facilitate political and economic integration to the West by strengthening cooperation and trade between its members. It operates within the framework of a *Central European Free Trade Agreement* (CEFTA).

Frameworks (CSF) for single Objective 1 regions (outside the regions of Prague and Bratislava, which were classified as Objective 2).

During the negotiations with the Commission on the strategies for implementing the structural funds for the period 2004-2006[7], this process continued with the creation of a limited number of regional and sectoral *operational programmes*.

In addition, if one considers the result of the negotiations that took place for the four countries mentioned above, the strategies are mainly focussed on sectoral actions (industry and businesses, infrastructure, development of human resources, rural development and agriculture). The regional dimension forms part of the programmes that cover all the areas with Objective 1 status, i.e., in most cases, countries rather than regions. The only devolved regions to benefit as such from an integrated territorial approach are the regions of Prague and Bratislava, for which Single Programming Documents (SPD) were drawn up. For other, geographically smaller candidate countries, the option of SPDs was retained to cover the whole of the countries' territory (Objective 1 and Objective 3).

This situation puts the regional and territorial dimension of European structural aid and raises the question of the ability of countries in transition to take firm action to even out regional disparities. Although the EU has encouraged the creation of local and regional authorities, regional action continues to be hampered by a severe lack of organisation within the economic fabric and the weakness of the new local authorities.

At the same time, whilst governments are making every effort to extol the virtues of EU enlargement, the populations of struggling regions cannot help but notice that unemployment rates remain high, public services are getting more expensive, and social services are getting worse.

It is certainly the case that European aid brings in sufficient resources for revitalising some of the economic fabric of these countries, but as stated by the Commission with reference to the various national plans for regional development, one of the main objectives of the programmes that have been put in place is to increase the level of national GDP. It would therefore be more accurate to talk about regional convergence

---

[7]   These negotiations between the candidate countries and the European Commission ended in December 2003.

on a central European scale rather than territorial cohesion between prosperous areas and crisis-hit ones. This approach, incidentally, is confirmed by the recent guidelines promoted as part of the Lisbon Agenda.

With regard to economic and social cohesion and territorial policies proper, it is necessary to keep in mind that, in the EU15, public expenditure accounts for 47% of national GDP. This figure shows the significant role that national redistributive policies can play in reducing disparities between regions. For the countries of central and eastern Europe, the main thing is to find the right level of European aid and to differentiate between structural aid for transition on the one hand, and aid that can help, as one of a number of tools that remain to be invented, the socio-economic integration of all the regions.

What place should the countries of central and eastern Europe have in European cohesion policy?

On the financial level, the attitude of the EU15 countries is not exactly favourable to increasing the EU's budget for the benefit of the countries of central and eastern Europe. First of all, the Fifteen decided, in Autumn 2002, to freeze expenditure on the CAP until 2013. Next, the Heads of State and Government of six countries – Germany, the United Kingdom, the Netherlands, Austria, Sweden and France – requested in December 2003 that the EU budget be limited to 1% of European GDP, which was the level it reached in 2003 before enlargement.

However, the European Commission, in its proposed budget for the next programming period (2007-2013) believes that such restrictions are rather unrealistic given the needs generated by the arrival of ten countries of central and eastern Europe. The College of Commissioners chaired by Romano Prodi has proposed that the European budget be increased by one-third, rising progressively from €116 billion in 2006 (1.11% of European GDP) to €143.1 billion in 2013 (1.14% of European GDP).

The guidelines currently favoured by the Commission follow logically from the guidelines set out in the Lisbon and Gothenburg agendas: to ensure that the EU becomes the most competitive and dynamic knowledge-based economy in the world whilst maintaining its economic and social cohesion and ensuring careful management of its natural resources. These guidelines are among those developed in the Priorities for the enlarged European Union published by the Commission in February 2004[8].

The challenge for European political leaders is to respond to the drop in European growth and to the poor productivity gains that have been evident in the European economy for several years, and to develop a growth policy that also takes into account the difficulties of the economically weakest geographical areas and industrial sectors. However, funds to promote "competitiveness for growth and employment" explicitly refer to the Lisbon agenda and are essentially aimed at strengthening Europe's economic potential[9]. From this point of view, the purpose of the funds will be to prioritise on those sectors and regions that excel in innovation, research or education.

On that subject, and without entering into the debates that surrounded the Sapir report[10], one could ask whether the small EU budget is capable of breathing new life into the whole continent's economy. This is above all a political project that will require coordinated commitment from all the governments. Conversely, geographically-based action in favour of crisis-hit areas could be carried out coherently at sub-national level. They have the advantage of making Europe more visible to those who have the most to fear from the opening of borders, which is essential to the pursuit of the European project.

In parallel with these competitiveness goals, the European Commission presents a revamped cohesion policy, which also takes its inspiration from the priorities set out at Lisbon. As Michel Barnier stated in his presentation of the Third Cohesion Report[11], the aim is to "reduce disparities in order to accelerate growth. Growth and cohesion are two sides of the same coin". European funds should not merely enable struggling regions to catch up where they are lagging behind. They must also promote the economic growth of Europe as a whole.

---

[8]   *Building our Common Future, Policy Challenges and Budgetary Means of the Enlarged Union 2007-2013*, Communication from the Commission to the Council and the European Parliament, Commission of the European Communities, Brussels, 10 February 2004 – COM(2004) 101 final.

[9]   The commitment appropriations for *Competitiveness for Growth and Employment* are €133 billion over the period 2007-2013.

[10]   André Sapir (Chairman), *An Agenda for a Growing Europe, Making the EU Economic System Deliver*, European Commission, Brussels, July 2003.

[11]   *A new partnership for cohesion - convergence, competitiveness, cooperation*, Third report on economic and social cohesion, European Commission, Brussels, February 2004.

Given its desire that "change[s] stemming from the new international division of labour are systematically incorporated *from the outset* into the design of all national and regional development strategies"[12], the challenge for the European Union will above all be to avoid a widening of this division between the East and the West of the continent.

From a spatial point of view, the Commission proposes to replace the current three Objectives of regional policy with objectives of *convergence, competitiveness* and *territorial cooperation*. The aim here is to "boost… economic performance overall at the same time as reducing economic and social disparities".

The first objective, which can be compared to the old Objective 1, concerns the less developed Member States and regions of the enlarged Union. This is aimed at the new Member States and at some regions of the EU15 hit by the statistical effect. This objective takes up the largest part of the funding, some 78% of the €336 billion budget for cohesion policy over the period 2007-2013. By adding the cohesion funding available for countries whose GDP does not exceed 90% of the Community average, this objective is the hard core of the fight against territorial disparities. Although the countries of central and eastern Europe will be able to claim no more than half of the funding set aside for cohesion policy[13], the main challenge for these countries will be to be capable of absorbing all the funds that are set aside for them.

The competitive objective overlaps with the strategic guidelines of Lisbon in several places. It is aimed at territories that are not covered by the convergence objective and thus excludes most of the regions of central and eastern Europe. On the one hand, a *regional* aspect aims to help regions to anticipate and promote economic change in certain areas (industrial, urban and rural areas). On the other, *national programmes* consist of more general action to promote employment. As the Commission states, interventions need to concentrate on a limited number of strategic priorities, where they can provide added value and have a multiplier effect on national or regional policies. This objective is consistent with the actions to promote "competitiveness for growth and employment" mentioned above.

---

[12] COM(2004) 101 final, op cit, p18.

[13] The countries of central and eastern Europe will be able to receive funding up to a maximum of 4% of their GDP. The EU believes that these countries would not be able to absorb greater sums than this.

Thirdly, *the objective of territorial cooperation* on a cross-border and transnational basis puts the emphasis on exchanges between states by taking advantage of "border effects". However, these areas of the EU are relatively strong economically, and need to address issues of strategic development rather than economic and social cohesion.

Decisions on the budget and the reform of structural aid have not yet been taken and will continue to be the subject of tough negotiations. From a financial point of view, the new members, who represent one fifth of the surface area and the population of the EU, have been promised some €40.5 billion in commitment appropriations between 2004 and 2006. That represents less than 15% of the €300 billion budget for the 25 as a whole over the same period. However, it is unlikely that actual payments over this period will reach 30% of that sum. This situation raises the worrying prospect that these countries will be net contributors. Whilst it is difficult to assess their level of spending, it is already laid down that they will have to contribute €16.2 billion to the Community budget over the period 2004-2006. However, there is provision for a compensation mechanism so that those countries in economic difficulty will not immediately become net contributors to the European budget.

Beyond this, if the countries of central and eastern Europe cannot really influence the amounts that are set aside for them, they can nonetheless have a say in the reorganisation of methods of intervention so that they can make best possible use of these funds. If that is to be achieved, it is essential that the countries develop ambitious accompanying strategies to support those running projects and to increase their chances of success.

In fact, it would appear essential to reform European policy so that, in a Europe of 25, all the members are able to differentiate clearly between matters that come under their own competencies (regional development) and matters that could fall within the remit (which remains to be specified) of the EU. It could be a specific competency in town and country planning, support for infrastructure on a continental scale, which is currently enshrined in the cross-border policy of the INTERREG Community initiative, by setting up trans-European communications networks and, in particular, by the drawing up of the European Spatial Development Perspective (ESDP).

On the territorial level, in the face of continuous change within economies and societies, and of worsening divisions in both urban and rural areas, Europe must maintain the means to intervene through aid targeted at particular regions. This could be based on the model of the Community initiative programmes, which currently make it possible to carry out actions in clearly identified territories and on multi-sectoral themes (rural or urban areas, employment aid). Whilst keeping a certain distance from the regionalised method of programming and allocation of funds, the idea would above all be to raise the profile of Europe's intervention in struggling areas that are likely to feed Euroscepticism.

Conclusion

European regional policy, as designed in favour of backward or structurally disadvantaged areas, has to some extent raised the profile of the European institutions. It is also true that today's Europe is being built broadly through the major regions, trade, and cooperation in research and higher education. It is crucial that these fields of action be strengthened in order to increase Europe's economic potential in the face of global competition.

It is also important to build a political project and to demonstrate overall consistency at this key time in European history. Once the EU expands to include the countries of central and eastern Europe, territorial disparities will be greater than ever before, and one could ask whether the EU has the political will to reorganise itself at the centre. By further strengthening its strongest economic sectors and territories, is the EU giving itself the means quickly to reduce the division between the East and West of the continent, as it claims its wants to do as part of its integration into the world economy?

In this context, the countries of central and eastern Europe are faced with the need to modernise their economies whilst limiting the social effects of transition. In the race for strategic investment, the territorial aspect is partially taken into account, if only in that the importance of communication networks and of the effects of urbanisation are recognised. For each of the countries of central and eastern Europe, the challenge is both to influence a European political structure that will not be able to meet all their expectations and to equip themselves with the necessary human, methodological, institutional and financial means to draw up their own model for society.

Patricia Schläger-Zirlik, Bayreuth University

The learning region strategy in urban and regional development

1. Introduction

Over the last few years, the idea of learning as a strategy has become fashionable. It has been applied in contexts such as "training offensives", "learning enterprises and organisations", and also on the level of regions. In the context of eastwards enlargement by the EU and the issues connected with bringing the EU regional economies into line with each other, regional learning processes can make a decisive contribution to rapid adaptation to new conditions.

The following paper[1] begins with a brief explanation of the theoretical basis of the learning region strategy before going on to discuss possible ways of identifying regional learning processes. The aim is to show how learning works in social systems, how learning or learning processes can be identified and recorded within (regional) systems and which institutional and situational conditions can influence learning in the regional context. The empirical case study of introducing city marketing activities in four selected cities in transition countries is described. Finally, these practical experiences and the preceding theoretical discussion are used to derive basic conditions for successful regional learning processes.

2. The learning region strategy- theoretical basis

The learning region strategy is a transdisciplinary concept based on the findings of developmental psychology, sociology, and management studies which reflects the significance of learning processes in regional development. The learning region strategy is one of the models of endogenous concepts in which regional transformation shaped by the regional actors themselves replaces externally controlled programmes

---

[1] The dissertation which this paper is based on has already been published as Schläger-Zirlik, P. (2003): Der Ansatz der Lernenden Region am Beispiel der Übertragung des Stadtmarketinggedankens auf ausgewählte Städte in Transformationsländern. - Vol. 220, Working Materials on Environmental Planning and Development, Bayreuth, and also online at http://opus.ub.uni-bayreuth.de/volltexte/2003/32/index.html

characterised by hierarchical structures, subsidies, and intervention. At the heart of this approach is promotion of intra-regional cooperation, networking, and collaboration to develop strategies which offer appropriate solutions reflecting specific local circumstances through regional systems of innovation[2]; in other words, it aims to make the best possible use of regionally available potential. The necessary empowerment of regional actors (personnel, social, methodological and specialist resources) is based on the existence of learning processes.

Learning starts with the individual. There is no unified theory of learning capable of resolving all the contradictions between various research on the subject. The main schools of thought are behaviourism (including Pavlov/classical conditioning), cognitivism (e.g. Piaget/developmental psychology or Gagné/hierarchical learning structures[3]) and social cognitive theories of learning (mainly represented by Bandura in the 1970s[4]). All of these are based on the idea that all perceptions are individually interpreted and examined for compatibility with existing patterns of experience. Previous experiences function as a filter, causing path-dependency of learning processes.

In a social context, individual learning can also be accompanied by group learning. A number of ideas on the subject of learning in social systems have been put forward, for example in sociological and management studies literature[5]. Of these, theories of "organisational learning", which describe the creation of skills and reciprocal use of common codes for the transfer and reception of experience-based knowledge, have most often been applied on regional levels[6].

In the debate on regional policy, "learning" or the ability to learn is seen as a rapid collective response to a fast changing environment. Very diverse interpretations of the concept of the learning region can be found in the literature on the subject[7]; for the

---

[2]   Cf. for example Cooke et al (2003): Regional Innovation Systems, and Lundvall et al (2000): National systems of production, innovation and competence building.

[3]   Piaget (1985): Meine Theorie der geistigen Entwicklung; Gagné (1980): Die Bedingungen des menschlichen Lernens.

[4]   Bandura (1979): Sozial-kognitive Lerntheorie. Stuttgart.

[5]   Miller (1986): Kollektive Lernprozesse.

[6]   Cf. for example Argyris / Schön (1985): Organizational Learning; Fiol / Lyles (1985): Organizational Learning; Probst / Büchel (1994): Organisationales Lernen; Senge (1998): Die fünfte Disziplin.

[7]   Cf. for example Oinas / Virkalla (1997): Learning, Competitiveness and Development, Hassink (1997): Die Bedeutung der Lernenden Region für die regionale Innovationsförderung, and Scheff (1999):

sake of a systematic overview, work on the subject can be classified into three basic approaches:

- the human capital-oriented approach, which focuses on individual learning or regional training opportunities[8]. According to this approach, systematic linking of the various groups of actors from production to targeted training to joint research and development activity improves conditions for all participants;

- the innovation-oriented approach, which basically involves targeted development and networking of small and medium-sized regional enterprises[9]. A high concentration of cooperation within a value chain or a cluster necessarily leads to dissemination and utilisation of experience across several companies;

- the environment-oriented approach, according to which a new programming culture together with the establishment and optimisation of regional networks contribute to learning processes[10].

A review of the literature makes it clear that there are various preconditions for implementing the concept of a learning region, such as the willingness of individual actors to learn, the willingness of regional decision-makers to learn, an agreed model for regional actors to follow, and various other basic conditions. However, the learning region strategy has little or nothing to say on the question of how these basic conditions could be provided. The concept is therefore less useful as a self-contained regional policy instrument (although the initiation of learning processes of course has an important role to play in many regional development strategies, and some individual aspects are certainly a very productive addition to the range of options available to regional policymakers) than on account of its potential for explaining regional learning and innovation processes.

Lernende Regionen - Regionale Netzwerke als Antwort auf globale Herausforderungen; Butzin (2000): Netzwerke, Kreative Milieus und Lernende Region.

[8] Blessin (1997): Von der lernenden Organisation zur lernenden Region; Florida (1995): Toward the Learning Region.

[9] Morgan (1997): The Learning Region: Institutions, Innovation and Regional Renewal; Malmberg / Sölvell / Zander (1996): Spatial Clustering, Local Accumulation of Knowledge and Firm Competitiveness; Oinas / Virkalla (1997): Learning, Competitiveness and Development.

[10] Maier / Obermaier (1999): Kreative Milieus und Netzwerke.

3.   **Ways of identifying regional learning processes, illustrated by an empirical case study**

How can learning processes within a region be identified? What options are there for measuring learning in the regional context? These questions were investigated empirically by observing learning processes in the course of the INTERREG II C Project (96/C200/07) on City marketing as an innovative strategy for city development in Central and Eastern Europe. A two-year research project was carried out by the Economic Geography and Regional Planning Department at Bayreuth University in cooperation with the Geography faculties of the universities of Bratislava in Slovakia, Maribor in Slovenia, Pécs in Hungary, and Plzeň in the Czech Republic to introduce city marketing strategies in these four cities.

The empirical analysis was based on the following assumptions:

- The theory of learning can be applied to learning processes in urban systems. Due to the power structures existing in cities, learning will be a top-down process. When ideas penetrate public consciousness and the number of individual learners/multipliers starts to rise sharply, the system as a whole learns too. However, this learning process can encounter resistance and come into conflict with established practices, power structures and procedures.

- In the past, urban development in transition countries was determined by the political doctrine of building socialist cities. After the political and economic changeover, this political doctrine was replaced by democratic processes and economic pressures. The transition process is therefore a relearning process, as old ways of thinking need to be overcome and replaced with new value systems, all of which can only happen over a longer period.

- Cities in transition countries are capable of learning and can also benefit by learning from the experiences of other countries. In social systems, of which cities are an example, learning processes can be identified by observing communication and interaction and the environment in which they take place.

During the research project, the city marketing process went through the classical stages: a situational analysis, an analysis of strengths and weaknesses, formulating a vision, working out a model and objectives for future development, and finally, deriving strategies and specific measures. It was assumed that a holistic city marketing programme operating under normal conditions was an appropriate context for initiating learning processes in an urban system, firstly because introducing a city marketing programme means changes to organisational procedures within a city which first have to be "learned", secondly because the city marketing process is intrinsically determined by and dependent on learning, and thirdly because running the project in parallel in five cities with an ongoing exchange of experiences is conducive to the processes of "learning from others" and "learning together" as well as direct comparison of the various outcomes.

The theory of learning was used to identify three levels on which learning processes could take place and on which the introduction of a city marketing programme could be analysed within individual cities:

- on the micro-level, i.e. on the level of those participating directly in the project, in terms of individual learning,

- on the meso-level, i.e. on the level of working groups in the context of an holistic city marketing process, in terms of collective learning,

- on the macro-level, i.e. on the level of the city, depending on the extent to which networking occurs between the various working groups, and the extent to which the idea of city marketing is actually adopted by decision-making mechanisms.

For each of these levels several dimensions were studied, the specific development of which was indicative of the quality of learning processes and whether such processes were taking place. The method used to investigate such processes was to ask individuals participating directly in the project qualitative questions and also to conduct interviews between experts and individual representatives of all four cities. The processes under observation were then compared with "ideal outcomes" which had been formulated in the preliminary stages of the project, enabling conclusions to be drawn on the extent to which learning had progressed.

On the micro-level, i.e. on the level of individual participants in the project, it was possible to identify learning processes with the help of measurement criteria developed during the project, but there was no actual implementation of a genuine holistic city marketing process in the course of the project, since other local actors in the particular cities did not become involved (ultimately, the groups to which the project was addressed were unwilling to cooperate). Because of this, no learning processes were observed on the macro- and meso-levels, i.e. in terms of group training and skills acquired by groups during the project. One of the reasons was the lack of conviction on executive levels that the city marketing programme was an effective strategy for overcoming current problems. In addition, many local decision-makers were unaware of the project. In this project, the university acted as a catalyst for ideas on the level of local politics. This role was new for the university, given that its position as an institution acting within and for the region has not yet been sufficiently established. Besides, to some extent there were already specific city marketing activities in all of the four cities, and therefore political decision-makers in transition countries were already familiar with the idea of thinking and acting in terms of competition. Economic pressures and the employment situation have in particular made it necessary to compete for investment. However, the case study demonstrates that there is still a long way to go in terms of involvement by ordinary citizens and their desire to participate in shaping future urban development.

Nevertheless, city marketing programmes remain an intrinsically suitable context for initiating learning processes in an urban system which can be identified and observed using the criteria developed in the methodological section of this study. Furthermore, some aspects of the experiences of the INTERREG project can help to identify factors determining whether regional learning processes can be successfully induced. No doubt, the fact that very little in the way of learning processes was observed in the empirical case study had partly to do with the fact that many such "success factors" were lacking or only present to a limited extent in the cities participating in the project.

At the beginning of the project it was thought that, whereas in western countries a market-economy-oriented approach by government authorities can draw on a very long tradition of corporate marketing, transition countries are only at the beginning of slow and gradual progress in this direction. However, this opinion was not borne out by observations during the INTERREG project. In all four participating cities some thought had already been given to marketing activities even before the beginning of the project. However, in terms of objectives and content, marketing obviously focuses on areas where the city itself stands to gain financially. As a result, the emphasis is on marketing aimed at tourists and investors from outside the city. Activities targeted at local entrepreneurs and residents can only be observed in situations where, for example, there is an urgent need for action due to young, well-qualified individuals with specialist skills tending to move away from a city.

Whereas mayors are seen in all four cities as the main driving force for urban development, employees of municipal authorities are more often perceived by the public as "bureaucrats" than as "managers". Such perceptions often lead to communication problems and mutual scepticism between institutions and individual actors within cities. In many cases several organisations pursue similar goals but without cooperating.

It is hardly possible to initiate a holistic city marketing process if local decision-makers and especially mayors are not convinced of its value. It seems that initiatives by ordinary citizens or local entrepreneurs such as those common in many German cities play much less of a role in transition countries. One of the reasons is that, for example, city-centre retail activity is not yet seen as a factor which shapes the image of the city. Another reason is that ordinary citizens of transition countries are not yet particularly inclined to participate in the development of their cities. In view of this, top-down processes seem more likely to succeed, but these would require decision-makers who are acceptable to a broad majority and are themselves convinced of the value of city marketing as a strategy.

In many cities in transition countries, the most pressing issues are the lack of funding and competition for jobs. Even more so than their western counterparts, political decision-makers focus on re-election and show little interest in activities whose effects will only become apparent in the long term. At the same time, the feeling of being dependent on decisions by central government clearly tends to inhibit individual initiative. There is no doubt that city marketing will therefore focus on individual areas where activity is possible and feasible despite the scarcity of funding, and generates measurable benefits (e.g. increases in the number of tourists, number of jobs created, etc.), and areas where many actors can be persuaded to collaborate.

In this sense, the situation with regard to city marketing activities is not so very different to that of German cities. Although only a small number of cases was studied, the impression arises that municipal authorities in transition countries are already familiar with marketing (or at least outdoor advertising activities), competition, and a competition-oriented approach. If one bears in mind that a little over ten years ago a very different system of values was in place, one can see that very significant learning processes have taken place over the last few years.

In all four of the cities observed in the project, there was a great deal of optimism about membership of the European Union. However, political decision-makers in the cities participating in the INTERREG project did not rate the value of contacts or exchange of experiences with other cities as envisaged by the project very highly. In addition, there were only a few instances of institutions and organisations within the same city or in different cities collaborating as partners, with the exception of international links between twin towns, which however were generally only of a formal character and did not involve any exchange of specialist knowledge. During the project, no communication or interaction relating to city marketing was identified within the social system by empirical investigation. However, there has been a noticeable change in objectives and a strategic reorientation of town planning compared with the objective of building a socialist city which was pursued before the political and economic changeover. Each of the cities observed in the case studies had formulated some kind of a strategy for defining the identity of the city within national and to some extent also international urban systems.

4.   Conditions for regional learning processes to succeed

The following basic conditions for successful regional learning processes can be derived from the preceding theoretical discussion and practical experiences:
- For enhanced cooperation and output, both individuals and groups/social systems need to have **feedback** on the quality of their performance/cooperation or the results of their activity. For learning to take place through feedback, indicators need to be previously defined as a basis for assessing the progress of learning. For this reason, it is helpful for the learning process to be broken down into smaller units which are as clear as possible, so that the results of learning become apparent with as little delay as possible. Feedback is a kind of monitoring process which can be used to assess whether objectives have been achieved (comparison of target and actual results) and also if the objectives are still appropriate (assessment of target results).

- **Anticipation by individuals of their environment and self-reflection** are closely connected with feedback. Clear perception of one's environment can reveal where problems are likely to occur (early warning system) and encourage more effective activity (benchmarking). However, in the case of complex phenomena, adopting or imitating a model can often be of doubtful value. Value systems cannot simply be adopted, as shown by the slowness of the process of adapting to the market economy in transition countries.

- **Intensive interaction and communication** in the context of an appropriate culture of discussion is essential for learning processes in social systems to take place. For feedback and anticipation of the environment to be effective, they must be accompanied by an intensive exchange of experiences within a social system.

- Learning in social systems requires **pressure for change** on the one hand and **willingness to change**, i.e. openness to innovation, on the other. Learning and change must be seen as positive concepts.

- In order to initiate a pre-defined process (model), there is a need for decision-makers (the power elite) to lend their support and to introduce change top-down. On the other hand, if the aim is to encourage a general search for individual approaches, organisational research suggests that networked and decentralised structures with flat hierarchies are more conducive to success.

- Jointly formulated specific objectives (a target vision) can make a significant contribution to stimulating voluntary cooperation. A **goal- and results-oriented approach** is also an important aspect of feedback as described above.

These "basic conditions" can be used to identify various factors which can enable or promote learning processes, and the absence of which may prevent learning processes from succeeding. The main practical relevance of these findings is that they provide criteria which can be taken on board at the very start of formulating (regional) learning processes. However, it is unclear to what extent they could be planned or applied to situations in other regions. In view of the current challenges which cities and regions are facing in an increasingly competitive environment, their ability to learn will certainly play an increasingly important role in the future.

5.   Conclusion

Political decision-makers in cities in transition countries are already familiar with the idea of thinking and acting in terms of competition. In particular, economic pressures and the employment situation have made it necessary for cities to compete for investment. However, the case study demonstrates that there is still a long way to go in terms of involvement by ordinary citizens and their desire to participate in shaping future urban development. In this context, the "success factors" for the initiation of learning processes discussed in the thesis could be used as indicators and support in planning the details of future projects.

Of course, the preceding observations are not fully representative of other situations, and cannot be used to derive conclusions which are fully applicable to other cities. The investigation has also raised some new questions, for example: how committed are regional actors to long-term action? What form should regional leadership of regional change take? Who actually initiates learning processes? However, the findings may be useful for initiating other learning processes (in transition countries), if they are applied to assessment of the analysis and design of learning processes. It is clear from the "success factors" identified here that "regional learning" is not a process which leads to a definite conclusion, and also that there is no ready-made solution which can guarantee the success of regional learning.

Selected bibliography

Argyris, C. / D. A. Schön (1985): Organizational Learning. A Theory of Action Perspective, Reading (Mass.).

Bandura, A. (1979): Sozial-kognitive Lerntheorie. Stuttgart.

Blessin, B. (1997): Von der lernenden Organisation zur lernenden Region. Discussion Papers 8/1997 of the Europäische Forschungsstelle für den ländlichen Raum (European Research Centre for Rural Areas), Stuttgart.

Butzin, B. (2000): Netzwerke, Kreative Milieus und Lernende Region: Perspektiven für die regionale Entwicklungsplanung? – In: Zeitschrift für Wirtschaftsgeographie, vol. 3 / 4 2000, pp. 149-166.

Cooke, P. et al (2003): Regional Innovation Systems, 2nd edition, London.

Fiol, C. M. / M. A. Lyles (1985): Organizational Learning. - In: Academy of Management Review, vol. 10, pp. 803-813.

Florida, R. (1995) Toward the Learning Region. – In: Futures 27, pp. 527-536.

Gagné, R. M. (1980): Die Bedingungen des menschlichen Lernens, 5th edition, Hanover.

Hassink, R. (1997): Die Bedeutung der Lernenden Region für die regionale Innovationsförderung. - In: Geographische Zeitschrift vol. 2+3 / 97, pp. 159-173.

Lundvall et al (2000): National systems of production, innovation and competence building. – In: Research policy, 31, pp. 213-231.

Maier, J. / F. Obermaier (1999): Kreative Milieus und Netzwerke – neue Erklärungs- und Strategieansätze der Regionalentwicklung sowie deren empirische Überprüfung anhand von Fallstudien in Bayern. – Final report of the research project for the "Technologischer Wandel und Regionalentwicklung in Europa 1997-1998" German Research Foundation Priority Programme, Bayreuth.

Malmberg, A. / Ö. Sölvell / I. Zander (1996): Spatial Clustering, Local Accumulation of Knowledge and Firm Competitiveness, - In: Geografiska Annaler 78 B, pp. 85-97.

Miller, M. (1986): Kollektive Lernprozesse. Studien zur Grundlegung einer soziologischen Lerntheorie. Frankfurt am Main.

Morgan, K. (1997): The Learning Region: Institutions, Innovation and Regional Renewal. - In: Regional Studies, vol. 31.5, pp. 491-503.

Oinas, P. / S. Virkalla (1997): Learning, Competitiveness and Development; Reflections on the Contemporary Discourse on "Learning Regions". - In: Eskelinen, H. [Ed.]: Regional Specialisation and Local Environment - Learning and Competitiveness. Stockholm, pp. 263-277.

Piaget, J. (1985): Meine Theorie der geistigen Entwicklung, Frankfurt.

Probst, G. / B. Büchel (1994): Organisationales Lernen, Wiesbaden.

Schläger-Zirlik, P. (2003): Der Ansatz der Lernenden Region am Beispiel der Übertragung des Stadtmarketinggedankens auf ausgewählte Städte in Transformationsländern. -Volume 220 of working materials on environmental planning and development, Bayreuth, and also online at http://opus.ub.uni-bayreuth.de/volltexte/2003/32/index.html.

Scheff, J. (1999): Lernende Regionen - Regionale Netzwerke als Antwort auf globale Herausforderungen, Graz.

Senge, P. M. (1998): Die fünfte Disziplin- Kunst und Praxis der lernenden Organisation. Stuttgart.

Shrivastava, P. (1983): Typology of Organizational Learning Systems. - In: Journal of Management Studies, vol. 20, pp. 7-28.

EUROPEAN UNION

**Committee
of the
Regions**

DECISION No. 229/03

**laying down technical and financial rules concerning the annual thesis
competition**

LOCAL AND REGIONAL AUTHORITIES IN THE EUROPEAN UNION

organised by the Committee of the Regions

THE SECRETARY-GENERAL

HAVING REGARD TO Council Regulation (EC, Euratom) No 1605/2002 of 25 June 2002 on the Financial Regulation applicable to the general budget of the European Communities[1];

HAVING REGARD TO Commission Regulation (EC, Euratom) No. 2342/2002 of 23 December 2002 laying down detailed rules for the implementation of Council Regulation (EC, Euratom) No. 1605/2002 of 25 June 2002 on the Financial Regulation applicable to the general budget of the European Communities[2],

HAVING REGARD TO the Rules of Procedure of the Committee of the Regions[3]

\

---

[1]   OJ L 248, 16.9.2002, p. 1.
[2]   OJ L 357, 31.12.2002, p. 1.
[3]   OJ L 189, 29.7.2003, p. 53.

HAVING REGARD TO the Decision of the Bureau of the Committee of the Regions of 13 November 1996 (DI/CdR 53/96 rev.) authorising the organisation of an annual thesis competition;

HAVING REGARD TO Regulation No. 235/2002 of the Bureau of the Committee of the Regions of 19 November 2002 on the refund of travel expenses and the payment of flat-rate travel and meeting allowances for members of the Committee of the Regions;

HAVING REGARD TO Decision No. 192/03 of the Bureau of the Committee of the Regions of 8 October 2003 appointing the acting secretary-general as delegated authorising officer;

WHEREAS:

(1)   since 1996, the Committee of the Regions (CoR) has engaged in dialogue with the European academic world by organising an annual doctoral thesis competition, "Local and regional authorities in the European Union";

(2)   to this end, it has laid down technical and financial rules on the organisation of this competition;

(3)   the role of local authorities within the European Union is arousing a growing interest beyond the borders of Europe, and so the Committee of the Regions has decided to open this competition to candidates who are not nationals of one of the EU Member States but who have obtained a doctorate from a university in these countries;

(4)   in view of the accession of ten new Member States on 1 May 2004, the Committee of the Regions plans to open this annual thesis competition to the nationals of these states;

(5)   the technical rules on the organisation of this competition must be modified accordingly and the financial rules must be harmonised with the provisions of Regulation No. 235/2002 of the Bureau of the Committee of the Regions on the refund of travel expenses and the payment of flat-rate travel and meeting allowances for members of the Committee of the Regions;

(6)   it is therefore necessary to repeal Decision No. 221/99 of the secretary-general of the Committee of the Regions of 28 October 1999 on the rules governing the annual thesis competition,

DECIDES AS FOLLOWS:

FIRST PART: TECHNICAL RULES

Article 1
Purpose of the competition

The purpose of the competition is to award an annual prize for doctoral theses (in the fields of law, economics, political science or sociology) on the role of local and regional authorities in the European Union. The list of the university diplomas recognised in each Member State of the European Union or the ten future Member States appears in Appendix I.

The subject of the competition shall be determined annually by the Bureau of the Committee of the Regions.

An independent selection board shall select the best or the two best theses deserving a prize.

A prize of €2,000 shall be awarded to the best thesis and, if appropriate, a prize of €1,000 shall be awarded to the second best thesis.

Article 2
Admission to the competition

The competition is open to nationals of one of the Member States of the European Union or of one of the ten future Member States and/or to the holders of a doctorate obtained at a university in an EU country.

Theses must be written in an official EU language. They must have been completed during the year in which the competition is announced, but must not have won a prize in any other competition.

Theses (**two copies**) must be accompanied by a summary presenting the thesis and demonstrating its relevance to the subject of the competition for that year. This summary (of not more than eight pages) must be written in one of the working languages of the selection board (English, French or German). Candidates must also provide a CV in one of these three languages.

Completed application files must be sent to the General Secretariat of the Committee of the Regions (Legislative Planning/Research Department, Rue Montoyer 92-102, B-1000 Brussels), postmarked not later than the closing date specified in the competition notice.

Supporting documents will not be returned, and will remain at the disposal of the CoR general secretariat.

Article 3
Selection of prizewinners

Preliminary selection

A preliminary selection will be made by a panel set up within the CoR general secretariat on the basis of the rules for admission to the competition. Theses that have been so selected will then be distributed to the various members of the selection board for assessment.

Membership of the selection board:

The selection board shall be appointed by the CoR president following a proposal by the secretary-general. It shall comprise academics from the different EU Member States and at least one CoR member or alternate.

The selection board shall be chaired by a CoR member or alternate.

The CoR general secretariat shall organise the work of the selection board.

Selection procedure

The procedure for selecting theses shall be in three stages during which each thesis shall be submitted for examination to the various members of the selection board.

In an initial stage, each of the theses shall be judged by a member of the selection board, who will have to write a report summarising the strong points and the weaknesses of the thesis and setting out the reasons why the thesis should receive a prize or not.

Each thesis shall then be the subject of a second assessment by another member of the selection board. He will also have to write an assessment and state the reasons why the thesis should receive a prize or not.

The following criteria in particular should be used as a guide by the selection board when assessing theses:

- the conformity of research with the annual topic of the competition;
- the taking into account of the territorial approach (local or regional) in the articulation of the thesis;
- the quality of the research;
- the capacity of analysis and of summary.

The selection board's members shall deliberate at a final meeting and decide from among the theses selected which should receive a prize. Before the selection board takes a final decision at this meeting, each of its members shall receive both the assessments on each of the theses.

The selection board shall take a decision by a vote. In the event of a tie, the chairman shall have a casting vote. If the chairman is absent, the chair shall be taken by the selection board's oldest member.

The selection board's decision shall be final.

The selection board reserves the right not to award a prize if none of the theses merits it, or to only award one prize.

Article 4
Presentation of the prizes

The prizes shall be formally presented by the CoR president at a plenary session. The presence of prizewinners is mandatory.

Article 5
Circulation of theses

Prizewinners undertake to authorise the CoR to reproduce their theses and circulate them among its members, and to authorise the reproduction and general circulation of the summaries of the theses.

SECOND PART: FINANCIAL RULES

I) REFUND OF EXPENSES INCURRED BY MEMBERS OF THE SELECTION BOARD AND PAYMENT OF ALLOWANCES

Article 6
Refund of travel expenses and payment of flat-rate allowances

The refund of the travel expenses and the payment of the flat-rate travel and meeting allowances of members of the selection board shall be carried out on the basis of the relevant provisions of Regulation No. 235/2002 on the refund of travel expenses and the payment of flat-rate travel and meeting allowances for members of the Committee of the Regions (Appendix II).

Article 7
Allowance for assessing doctorate theses

Each member of the selection board shall receive an allowance for each doctorate thesis that he assesses. The flat-rate amount of this allowance shall be €200.

Article 8
Postage expenses

Upon presentation of the relevant supporting documents, the Committee of the Regions shall refund all postage expenses incurred personally by selection board members.

II) REFUND OF EXPENSES INCURRED BY PRIZEWINNERS AND PAYMENT OF ALLOWANCES

Article 9
Refund of travel expenses and payment of flat-rate allowances

The refund of the travel expenses and the payment of the flat-rate travel and meeting allowances of prizewinners shall be carried out on the basis of the relevant provisions of Regulation No. 235/2002 on the refund of travel expenses and the payment of flat-rate travel and meeting allowances for members of the Committee of the Regions (Appendix II).

Refunds of travel expenses and the payment of allowances shall be limited to a total amount of €2,000 for each prizewinner.

Article 10
Procedures

The procedures for the refund of travel expenses and payment of flat-rate allowances pursuant to this decision shall comply with those laid down in Regulation No. 235/2002 on the refund of travel expenses and the payment of flat-rate travel and meeting allowances for members of the Committee of the Regions.

Article 11
Financial procedure

Before a meeting is convened and organised within the meaning of these rules, a proposal for the commitment of the relevant funds shall be made in accordance with the Financial Regulation. After the meeting the attendance list, duly signed, shall be forwarded to the general secretariat of the CoR.

Article 12
Final Provision

This decision cancels Decision No. 221/99 of the secretary-general of the Committee of the Regions of 28 October 1999 on the guidelines for the annual thesis competition.

Article 13
Entry into force

This decision shall enter into force on the day it is adopted.

Brussels, 17 November 2003.

(signed)
Gerhard Stahl
Acting Secretary-General

N.B.: Appendices overleaf.

*

*   *

APPENDIX I

Competition candidates must hold one of the following university degrees recognised in the Member States or future Member States of the European Union[1].

Germany:	Doktor (for example Dr. jur., Dr. phil.)
Austria:	Doktorat (for example Dr. iur., Dr. phil.)
Belgium:	Docteur/Doctor
Cyprus:	Doctor (PhD)
Denmark:	Ph.D. (since 1 September 1988)
Spain:	Doctor
Estonia:	Doktorikraad
Finland:	Tohtori (in Finnish), Doktor (in Swedish)
France:	Doctorat
Greece:	Didaktorikon diploma
Hungary:	Doctori Oklevél (PhD)
Ireland:	Doctor of Philosophy (Ph.D)
Italy:	Dottore di Ricerca (Dr.)
Latvia:	Doktors
Lithuania:	Daktaro Diplomas
Malta:	Doctor's Degree (PhD)
Netherlands:	Doctor (dr.)
Poland:	Doktor
Portugal:	Doutor
United Kingdom:	Doctor of Philosophy (Ph.D)
Slovakia:	Philosophiae Doctor (PhD)
Slovenia:	Doktorat
Sweden:	Filosophie doktor (fil. Dr) (ekonomie, juris etc.)
Czech Republic:	Doktor (PhD)

---

[1]

http://www.coe.int/T/E/Cultural_Co_operation/education/Higher%5Feducation/ENIC_Network/systemes.asp#TopOfPage

APPENDIX II

Committee
of the
Regions

REGULATION No. 235/2002

**on the refund of travel expenses and the payment of
flat-rate travel and meeting allowances for members of the Committee of the
Regions**

THE BUREAU OF THE COMMITTEE OF THE REGIONS,

HAVING REGARD TO the Treaty establishing the European Community, and in particular Articles 7, 263, 264 and 265 thereof;

HAVING REGARD TO the Protocol on the location of the seats of the institutions and of certain bodies and departments of the European Communities and of Europol, annexed to the Treaty of Amsterdam;

HAVING REGARD TO the Financial Regulation of 21 December 1977 applicable to the general budget of the European Communities, as amended, inter alia, by Council Regulation No. 1923/94 of 25 July 1994 and Council Regulation No. 2673/99 of 13 December 1999;

HAVING REGARD TO Commission Regulation EC No. 3418/93 of 9 December 1993 laying down detailed rules for the implementation of certain provisions of the Financial Regulation of 21

December 1977, as amended by Commission Regulation EC No. 1687/2001 of 21 August 2001;

HAVING REGARD TO   the Committee of the Regions Rules of Procedure and in particular Rules 35, 63(3) and 67 thereof;

HAVING REGARD TO   Decision No. 31/2000 of the Bureau of the Committee of the Regions of 15 February 2000 on the refund of travel expenses and the payment of daily subsistence and travel allowances,

HAS ADOPTED THIS REGULATION:

Article 1
Beneficiaries

1.   Members of the Committee of the Regions shall be entitled to refund of travel expenses in respect of their participation in the work of the Committee. They shall also receive flat-rate travel and meeting allowances, calculated in accordance with the terms and conditions laid down in these rules.

2.   Members shall, in respect of their attendance at meetings, seminars, conferences, etc. which are of particular interest to the Committee, be entitled to refund of travel expenses and payment of flat-rate travel and meeting allowances in accordance with the terms and conditions laid down in these rules, subject to submission of:

- an application in writing accompanied by the invitation to the event and the programme;
- the prior written authorisation of the President or, at his/her delegation, the Secretary General.

3.   Duly mandated alternates shall be entitled to refund of travel expenses and payment of flat-rate travel and meeting allowances on the same conditions as members, when replacing the latter. Members shall be entitled to only one refund of

travel expenses per meeting or plenary session, payable to either the member or his/her alternate.

4.   Where an alternate has been appointed as rapporteur, s/he shall be entitled to the refund of travel expenses and payment of flat-rate travel and meeting allowances provided for in these rules for his/her attendance at commission meetings or plenary sessions when the opinion for which s/he is rapporteur is on the agenda. This provision shall apply even when the member for whom s/he was acting as alternate at the time of his/her appointment as rapporteur is also present.

5.   Members attending a meeting of a political group of the Committee of the Regions held other than during the meeting days fixed for plenary sessions shall be entitled to the benefits provided for in these rules. Such extraordinary meetings shall be convened by the political group president. A duly mandated alternate shall be entitled to refund of travel expenses and payment of flat-rate travel and meeting allowances when replacing a member of the same political group, irrespective of the nationality of the alternate involved.

Article 2
Officially declared place of residence

1.   Both the refund of travel expenses and the calculation of flat-rate travel and meeting allowances shall be based on the distance between the officially declared place of residence and the venue of the meeting.

2.   The place of residence declared by the beneficiary on his or her appointment to the Committee shall be considered to be his or her officially declared place of residence (main place of residence). Any change shall be notified to the secretary-general and the imprest account office.

        If the member or alternate regularly works in another part of his or her Member State, s/he may submit to the secretary-general an application for recognition of a second official place of residence. The application must be accompanied by supporting documentation.

3.   Travel expenses shall be refunded on the basis of the most direct route between the officially declared place of residence and the venue of the meeting.

In the event that a beneficiary under these rules takes a longer or different route entailing additional costs compared with the cost of the direct route from the officially declared place of residence, the member or alternate shall submit to the secretary-general an application for prior authorisation (in accordance with Article 10), stating reasons and enclosing supporting documents showing the amount of the costs to be incurred.

4.   Travel expenses incurred by the president and the first vice-president of the Committee in fulfilling their duties may be refunded, even in cases where the journeys involved start from a point other than the declared place of residence.

5.   Members who change the details of their return journey, vis-à-vis the details notified to the imprest account office in respect of the route or ticket used, shall be obliged to submit a "change of journey" declaration on their return, by letter to the imprest account office, accompanied by supporting documentation.

Article 3
Refund of travel expenses

1.   **Travel by rail or by boat**

Rail or boat fares (up to a maximum of the first class fare, including supplements) actually paid shall be refunded on presentation of supporting documents.

The administration shall stamp the original travel document as proof of its presentation for reimbursement.

2.   **Travel by car**

In the case of travel by car, a person covered by these rules shall receive a refund at a flat rate of €0.20 per kilometre. The distance in kilometres between the meeting venue and the officially declared place of residence shall be determined by the administration by means of a computer program. In no case shall the amount refunded in respect of travel by car exceed the cost of a first class rail ticket for the same journey.

If two or more persons covered by these rules travel in the same car, the person responsible for the vehicle shall be entitled to the above refund, plus an additional payment of 20% in respect of each person accompanying him/her, provided s/he states their names in his expenses claim. The persons mentioned thereby forfeit any right to reimbursement of travel expenses for the corresponding part of the journey.

3. **Travel by air**

Air transport expenses actually paid shall be refunded on the basis of the cost of a ticket in the class below first class on production of the original flight ticket and boarding card (at least for the outward journey). The administration shall stamp the original travel document as proof of its presentation for reimbursement.

The use of "back-to-back" tickets must be declared in the expenses claim and original unused tickets returned to the imprest account office.

4. **Additional journeys**

If, for exceptional reasons, a second journey is made during a plenary session, or between two meetings held on two consecutive days, the member or alternate shall submit to the secretary-general an application for prior authorisation (in accordance with Article 10), stating reasons and enclosing supporting documents showing the amount of the costs to be incurred. Additional journeys of less than 100 km (one way) shall not be refunded.

5. **Travel expenses between the officially declared place of residence or meeting venue and the railway station, airport or port**

The foregoing provisions of Article 3 shall also apply to travel expenses between the officially declared place of residence or meeting venue and the railway station, airport or port.

For meetings held outside Brussels, travel by taxi from the station, airport or port to the meeting venue shall be eligible for refund upon application in writing to the secretary-general, stating reasons and enclosing supporting documents (in accordance with Article 10).

Article 4
Flat-rate travel allowance

1.   The flat-rate travel allowance shall cover all expenses incurred in the course of journeys.

2.   The flat-rate travel allowance shall be €117 per reference unit.

3.   The travel allowance shall be calculated in accordance with the table below at a flat rate based on the distance between the point of departure, the meeting venue and the place to which the beneficiary returns, irrespective of the means of transport used.

Journey distance	Corresponding number of reference units
from 0 km to 200 km	0
from 201 km to 400 km	0.75
from 401 km to 1,000 km	1
from 1,001 km to 2,000 km	1.5
over 2,000 km	2

In the case of journeys outside the European Union of more than 6,000 km, the flat-rate travel allowance for members shall be four reference units.

4.   If more than one consecutive meeting is attended at different venues, the allowance shall be calculated in accordance with the distance between the officially declared place of residence and the most distant meeting venue.

Article 5
Flat-rate meeting allowance

1.　　　　The allowance shall cover on a flat-rate basis all expenses at the meeting venue for a calendar day.

2.　　　　The daily allowance shall be €216.

3.　　　　The allowance shall be paid as follows:

(a)　for each day's participation in a meeting under the conditions set out in Article 1;

(b)　for each day intervening between two meetings when the person covered by these rules does not return to his/her declared place of residence, and provided that the total sum of this allowance does not exceed the total sum in respect of refund of travel expenses and allowances for travelling time which that person would have received if s/he had made the round trip from his/her initial place of departure and back. The beneficiary shall be required to provide evidence of the cost saving. This allowance shall under no circumstances exceed the equivalent of two daily meeting allowances;

c)　for each day on which there is no meeting during a plenary session as a result of cancellation or suspension of the proceedings, provided the claimant takes part in the work of the Committee or its constituent bodies on the preceding day and on the following day and provided s/he does not return to his declared place of residence in the interval;

d)　for an additional day if the meeting is scheduled for a Friday or a Monday, solely in order to enable the beneficiary to buy an economy air ticket (requiring a weekend stopover), and provided that this results in an overall cost saving (travel plus allowances) to the Committee. The beneficiary shall be required to provide evidence of the cost saving.

Article 6
Official visits

In the case of an official visit away from Committee headquarters, the president, or the vice-president who replaces the president, shall be entitled to refund of travel expenses (first class) and the flat-rate travel allowance, in accordance with the above Articles 3 and 4. They shall also be entitled to a double flat-rate meeting allowance for each day of attendance at meetings.

Article 7
Reimbursement procedure

1.   Members and alternates are obliged to sign the official attendance list at each meeting and/or on each meeting day.

2.   Expenses claim forms must be completed and signed by the entitled person during the meeting. Any claims submitted more than two weeks after the end of the meeting do not receive priority treatment. Claims for expenses requiring substantiation in the form of the travel document or other supporting documents cannot be considered unless they are accompanied by these documents.

The staff of the imprest account office, the authorised meeting ushers or persons responsible for the meeting are the sole persons authorised to receive these documents. If no duly authorised member of the administration is present, expense claims shall be submitted to the imprest account office. Claims must be accompanied by original transport documents and the relevant supporting documentation.

Article 8
Arrangements for payment of allowances and refund of travel expenses

1.   Allowances and refunds of travel expenses are calculated in euros.

2.   They are paid at the request of the person covered by these rules, by bank transfer to a bank or post office account. Any change in bank or post office

account details must be notified separately in writing to the secretary-general and to the imprest account office.

3.   Conversions of non-euro currencies is made at the exchange rate published monthly by the accounting officer of the European Commission (INFOR-EURO).

Article 9
Financial procedure

Before a meeting is convened and organised within the meaning of these rules, a proposal for the commitment of the relevant funds shall be made in accordance with the Financial Regulation and submitted before the meeting to the imprest account office, together with a list of the proposed participants, and the approval of the authorising officer. After the meeting the attendance list, duly signed, shall be forwarded to the imprest account office.

Article 10
Authorisation by the Secretary-General

The secretary-general shall be empowered to accept applications for recognition of a second official place of residence, in accordance with the provisions of Article 2(2).

The secretary-general shall be empowered to examine and accept applications for additional refunds, in accordance with the provisions of Articles 2(3), 3(4) and 3(5).

Article 11
Exceptional cases and/or cases not covered

Any exceptional cases and/or cases not covered by these rules shall be referred by the secretary-general to the president for decision.

Article 12
Final Provision

This regulation shall supersede Decision No. 31/2000 of the Bureau of the Committee of the Regions of 15 February 2000 on the refund of travel expenses and the payment of daily subsistence and travel allowances.

This Regulation shall enter into force on 1 January 2003.

The secretary-general shall be responsible for its implementation.

Brussels, 19 November 2002.

For the Bureau
of the Committee of the Regions

(signed)
Albert Bore
The President

———————————

Committee of the Regions of the European Union

COMMITTEE OF THE REGIONS THESIS COMPETITION
1996-2003

Luxembourg: Office for Official Publications of the European Communities

2004   232 pp.   16 x 23 cm

ISBN 92-895-0338-6